Remake it
Clothes

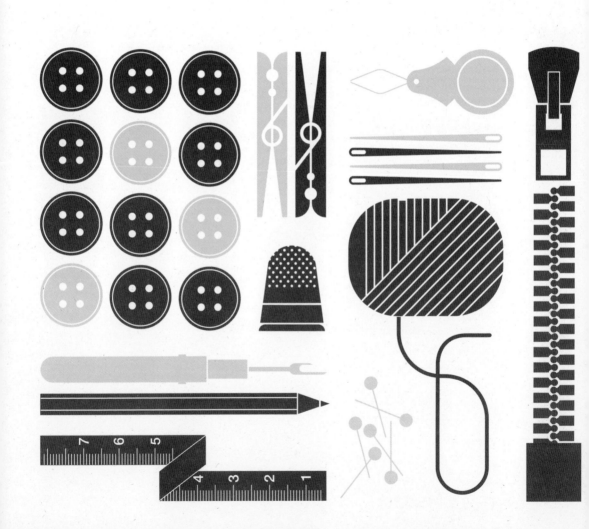

Remake it

Clothes

The essential guide to resourceful fashion
With over 500 tricks, tips and inspirational designs

Henrietta Thompson
Illustrations by Neal Whittington

Thames & Hudson

To Jubi, for being sew brilliant.

First published in the United Kingdom in 2012 by
Thames & Hudson Ltd, 181A High Holborn, London WC1V 7QX

Designed by Studio EMMI / www.emmi.co.uk

British Library Cataloguing-in-Publication Data
A catalogue record for this book is available from the British Library

ISBN 978-0-500-51632-4
Printed and bound in China by C&C Offset Printing Co. Ltd

To find out about all our publications,
please visit **www.thamesandhudson.com**.
There you can subscribe to our e-newsletter, browse or download
our current catalogue, and buy any titles that are in print.

Please note: the tips and instructions in this book are intended as
inspiration. The nature of this way of working means that the materials,
tools and outcomes of every project are likely to differ hugely depending
on your individual skill levels and the materials you have to hand,
and all projects involve some degree of risk. Although the author has
made every effort to ensure that the advice in this book is correct,
it is provided for general information only. Always read any relevant
manuals or instructions before using tools and chemicals and follow the
manufacturer's safety recommendations. The techniques suggested in
the book should not be used by anyone under 18 years of age. The Author
and Thames & Hudson accept no liability for any loss, damage or injury
arising as a consequence of the advice contained in this book.

Contents

A brief history of dressmaking at home

It is a common misconception that in order to make clothes it is important to be skilled at sewing. This may have been the case at one time, when dressmaking patterns were last in *Vogue* (and, if we are talking literally, that would have been in around 1961 when the fashion magazine sold its pattern distribution arm to Butterick), but since then the game has changed dramatically. Today, just as canny carpentry isn't the only way to craft a coffee table, fashioning a dress, a coat, or a hat is much more of a level playing field for tailors and amateurs than ever before. Advanced sewing techniques and pattern-cutting ability are useful, but they are not everything.

So what's changed? Fashion has had a phenomenal impact on the modern dressmaker's repertoire. In a matter of decades what constitutes acceptable dress has broadened and diversified to a point where now anything and everything goes. Since the middle of the last century, the front rows at fashion shows have witnessed punk, deconstructivism, grunge and every kind of retro revival and now, for the first time in history, clothing is frequently and deliberately ripped, frayed, distressed, rearranged and otherwise undone as a style statement. It is also fine to mix and match styles, fabrics, patterns and colours, to borrow garment types from any era or to mix them all at once, to choose hemlines, necklines, hat types, sleeves and scarves at random and assemble it all at will. This is the era of the individual: style is more a matter of education, talent and/or attention to detail than adhering to specific shapes and hemlines. Taste, meanwhile, is often considered to be overrated.

Besides this there have been huge enabling leaps in technology. Even beyond the invention of highly specialized machines, synthetic materials and Gaffer tape (the staple of every ad hoc artist's toolbox), working with textiles is very different from how it was 50 years ago. Today, much work can be achieved with a pair of scissors and a bit of imagination as we live in a time of many innovations: with, for example, new fabrics that don't require hemming and fastenings that don't require stitching.

When Mrs Sew-and-Sew made her first outing in the Make Do and Mend pamphlets that would be issued to every household in Britain in 1943, the clothes which were worn by men, women and children were to be clearly defined and ruthlessly dictated on a regular basis. Out of economy and necessity, home dressmaking was not so much commonplace as an expected activity of girls and women – and, with the outbreak of war, rationing and recession only made it more so. Darning socks was key to a happy household.

But with the onset of equal opportunities and industrial advances, mass production and high street chains came a cash-rich, time-poor society. Sewing skills have dwindled proportionately – the ability and wherewithal to whip up a wardrobe at home has become, if not rarefied, then certainly relegated to the status of hobby.

By contrast, today's new generation of dressmakers is motivated as much by a creative drive and ecological reasons as by economic ones. In fact, the numbers in which people – men and women – are defecting to a more homemade, handmade approach to dressing would point towards a much greater shift in the public psyche than a simple fashion trend. This time around the idea is appealing, not because it's fundamentally necessary but because it provides a counterpoint to the relentlessness of mass consumerism and disposable fashion. A homemade garment or accessory is a satisfying plate of soul-food at the kitchen table after decades of eating out every day.

The ethical and environmental arguments for upcycling clothing go beyond the well-documented benefits of reusing materials. Clothes that are handmade often tend to last – regardless of the expertness of their creation and the strength of the stitching, the dress made by your grandmother doesn't get thrown away quite as fast as its equivalent from Gap. The hand-me-downs, the fixed-up and the garments remade to measure hold memories somehow woven into their seams: the official buzzword is "emotional durability" and it's pretty powerful stuff.

The further afield and the further back in history we look, the more ingenious the ideas of reappropriation in dress. There is one book that describes how 4,000 years ago a couple of figleaves could be cunningly refashioned into undergarments, for example. For the Romans, meanwhile, a bed sheet might double as a party dress, while samurai warriors' sword-slashed kimonos might be reconfigured into a nice bag, purse, or other accessories. The indigenous peoples of South America have a knowledge of organic vegetal dyes that stretches back centuries, way before glorious Technicolor could bring such wild Western ways to the rest of the world.

The beauty of remaking clothes, as with upcycling for furniture and other accessories, is that half the work is often as simple as taking a fresh perspective and a broader view as to what might constitute a raw material. Carpet bags, fruitbowl fascinators and pillowcase skirts are just a few classic examples to which we're now well accustomed. From Vivienne Westwood to Martin Margiela, many a couturier has demonstrated the ability to create multiple new garments through a basic process of deconstruction. For the modern dressmaker, remaker and sartorial explorer, a pair of scissors and a knack for unpicking, boiling, folding, knotting and generally rearranging are all just as useful as the old Singer sewing machine.

Combining Garments, 1940s

Make Do and Mend, 1940s

Decades of deconstruction

Fashion is invariably a study of opposites and remaking trends in clothing are no exception. DIY practices have had a serious effect on fashion for a full century at least and in that time the practice has been claimed equally fiercely by wartime patriots and anarchists, Japanese minimalists and West Coast wasters. But whether their tools have been safety pins or psychedelic tie-dye skills, remaking has always been used to make a point.

Or to stage a revolution, as was the case with punk. The anti-fashion, anti-establishment movement, which first emerged in the mid-1970s across the UK and US alongside a loud, anarchist music score, was controversial and crude in attitude with wardrobes to match. In a move that was highly shocking at the time, all manner of unsuitable garb (usually found in charity and thrift shops) would be cut up and refashioned to attract maximum attention. This meant torn fabrics, frayed edges and ladders, and the addition of offensive slogans, studs and nails. Accessories included dog collars, lavatory chains, padlocks, razor blades and heavy utilitarian footwear. It was frightening.

When Vivienne Westwood and Malcolm McLaren signed up to the punk movement with their joint design ventures – the Sex Pistols music group and the SEX shop on the King's Road in London (which would sort the band members out with duly inappropriate wardrobes) – the style exploded further into the mainstream. In around 1977, British designer Zandra Rhodes began taking elements of the punk style and refining them to make them attractive to a more affluent, if still not exactly traditional, consumer, with bright colours and safety pins. Artfully distressed garments became luxurious with gold thread and embroidery and before too long the genre filtered its way into the mainstream, with people from all walks of life and of all ages sporting ripped seams and slogan T-shirts without a second thought to subverting any system at all.

Preceding punk in the 1960s, another subculture at the other end of the revolutionary spectrum had also been busy sewing their own for some time. The hippies had their own anti-corporation, anti-commercialism political statements to make via a DIY approach, but their weapons were peace, love and dip-dye. Natural, environmentally conscious fabrics and yarns were crafted into kaftans, fashioned into flares and flowing dresses, and seeds would be threaded into long swinging beaded necklaces. Individualistic styles epitomized the freedom and playfulness of the era.

While the hippies and punks were keeping up the craft contingent in the West during the 1980s, over in Japan, fashion's "Big Three" – Issey Miyake, Rei Kawakubo and Yohji Yamamoto – exploded controversially onto the scene, taking the Parisian approved acceptable norms of couture and turning them entirely upside down. In the process they exerted a huge influence on the possibilities for remaking. Fashion became an intellectual pursuit, with concepts such as wabi-sabi and "ma" manifest in androgynous, voluminous, folded and draped forms with raw edges and unfinished detailing – beauty was found in the deconstruction of traditional shapes and patterns.

In the 1990s, deconstructionism in fashion evolved again with a new phase, this time taking root in the US, where a youth disillusioned with their government and capitalism decided to make a statement – looking out for themselves. The grunge movement revived the DIY ethic by harnessing both hippie spirit and punk ideology, losing the free love and passionate fight for rights, and instead ending up with one (rather miserable) mash up of unkemptness. Again largely music motivated, its heroes would be the likes of Kurt Cobain and Courtney Love, while on the catwalks a young Kate Moss and her contemporaries modelled the controversial heroin-chic – ripped, stained and otherwise deliberately distressed garments in black, greys and khaki.

Fashion's obsession with vintage clothing crept up gradually, reaching its pinnacle in the first few years of this millennium. Retro, vintage and even antique garments became more readily available and much more in demand, thanks in no small part to the influence of models and actresses bucking the trend. A 1920s fur stole, a 1940s tea dress or a 1970s Afghan coat scores the wearer fashion points: unique, original and environmentally conscious, and·as high street fashion increasingly turned to history for inspiration, original vintage items could be a cheaper and/or more authentic way to achieve a designer look. Even high street chains and brands such as London's Topshop and Urban Outfitters would mark out dedicated areas of their stores for vintage concessions.

After struggling for years to be taken seriously by the fashion world, eco-designers finally saw the industry start to shift in their favour in the late noughties. Doubtless this began as a result of tireless campaigning by environmental fashion champions such as Orsola de Castro and Filippo Ricci, and the establishment (thanks largely to them) of various dedicated "green" fashion weeks such as "Esthetica", established in London in 2007.

A new remaking champion emerged – in 2007 Westwood launched the Active Resistance Manifesto against the "drug of consumerism", with a view to motivating people to act against climate change. She encouraged people to shop less and instead to create unique dresses from towels and curtains, to buy the best clothes that they could afford, and to wear them until they wear out: an incongruous statement from a fashion designer, maybe, and a controversial one.

From here the possibilities become interesting as designers start to work across disciplines and incorporate new technologies. Although so far we've seen only a handful of maverick minds (such as Hussein Chalayan and Alexander McQueen) push these ideas to interesting places, using and reusing elements and ideas from other industries could potentially open up exciting new possibilities in clothing. We are living in an era when almost anything goes and we have more choice, ability and knowledge than at any other time in history, but fashion's rule of opposites holds fast: when looking to the future our biggest resource is almost certainly always going to be our past.

Street Scene, London, 1970s

Good clothes open all doors

The national collection of textiles and fashion at the Victoria and Albert Museum in London is a walk-in wardrobe like no other. It covers a period of more than 2,000 years and holds an astonishing array of garments, with all manner of construction techniques and fabrics represented from all over the world. Although the V&A has collected both textiles and dress since its earliest days, the status of fashion within the decorative arts has only recently been considered worthy for consideration alone. Instead, only a garment of extraordinary fabric, innovative manufacture or, in rare cases, with a celebrated past owner would have justified a place in the museum's hallowed halls.

In the last few decades fashion has made huge leaps and today its importance as an artform is more widely recognized, and not just at the V&A. Dedicated fashion and textiles museums and museum collections have been established across the world in the past two decades. No longer can fashion be patronizingly dismissed as a mere people prettifier, a shallow symptom of capitalism, or a pastime useful only for filling untold vacancies in the female psyche. Instead, fashion is recognized as a powerful cultural force, an artform, a political tool and – if not quite an intellectual pursuit – then at least worthy of academic study. And, by the same thread, also worthy of investment.

The collecting of fashion – whether by institutions or individuals – is a phenomenon that emerged throughout the 20th century and continues to grow. While at one time it was an almost accidental pursuit, the preserve of actors and actresses, princes and princesses, society women and men – Grace Kelly, Audrey Hepburn, Wallis Simpson, Jackie Onassis – those whose style was admired and who made a point of it would naturally amass wardrobes of note. These days, however, collectors invest purely for the garment's design and historical value alone – whether or not they intend to wear a piece themselves.

Collecting jewelry and haute couture is much like collecting any other form of design – tangible value can be determined in their craftsmanship and precious materials. When it comes to other clothes and accessories, however, a more abstract sense of worth comes into play: history and provenance, individual quality, high-style design and detailing will all come to bear on an item's desirability in the market. And what this means is not only that there are certain items that should be carefully weighed up before taking the pinking shears to them, but also that as vintage and antique clothing becomes an increasingly popular investment choice, it has become a more complex one.

Online auctions such as eBay have made vintage and second-hand clothing and accessories much easier to trade, but hands-on experience counts for everything in this market. Specialist vintage fashion fairs, dealers and markets can provide this, as can viewings at auction houses. Tips about what to look for and avoid are as with any other antique market – it's crucial to check carefully for stains and flaws such as moth holes, scorches and tears, missing beadwork or embellishments. Carefully checking the label can reveal true dates as well as fakes to the specialist. Focusing on a particular period, designer or garment type allows for a more specialist knowledge and pieces that typify a designer's work will always fetch higher prices.

Dating garments has much to do with clues left by their manufacture: zips were not common in dresses until the post-war period, for example. Although some garments did feature zips in the 1930s (including plastic zips that were constructed with individual teeth like their metal counterparts) utility restrictions during the Second World War stopped their use. Most pre-war clothes were made by dressmakers and tailors and so did not feature labels, while washing care guidelines only became widespread in the 1970s. Machine overlocking of seams was popular from the 1960s and so can be an easy trick to tell the difference between copies and original garments.

Besides those pieces that demonstrate incredible handiwork and techniques of the pre-mass-production era, vintage classics that will provide enduring style and substance can be sourced from any decade. A 1950s Christian Dior dress, a 1960s Mary Quant shift, a 1970s Ossie Clark kaftan or a 1980s Giorgio Armani suit all define their time and yet retain their appeal no matter what current fashion trends come and go in the meantime. Likewise, items made famous by iconic wearers will fetch thousands: an off-the-shoulder Victor Edelstein dress worn by Princess Diana was sold at auction for $800,000 in 2011, the original Givenchy dress created for Audrey Hepburn in *Breakfast at Tiffany's* fetched £467,200 at Christie's in 2006. And those that mark iconic events, whether one-off or limited edition, can also raise serious funds, as was proven in 2011 when a rare 1979 Led Zeppelin concert T-shirt sold on eBay for $10,000. The seller might be pleased he hadn't succumbed to the need for a new tote bag and taken the scissors to it, although that would have been more rock and roll.

Wearing investment pieces is a controversial issue, and there are many who believe that collectable items ought not to be worn at all. Not to do so, to mummify a piece of history, is only slightly less perverse than a cellar full of vintage wines that never get drunk for want of an occasion special enough. They may have been painstakingly amassed at great expense, but clothes were designed to be worn, and it is only then that they can be made to come alive.

For Ascot, 1945

Christian Dior, 1947

WOMENSWEAR

Tops, dresses, skirts, trousers, blouses, leggings, lingerie, shorts, scarves and nightdresses

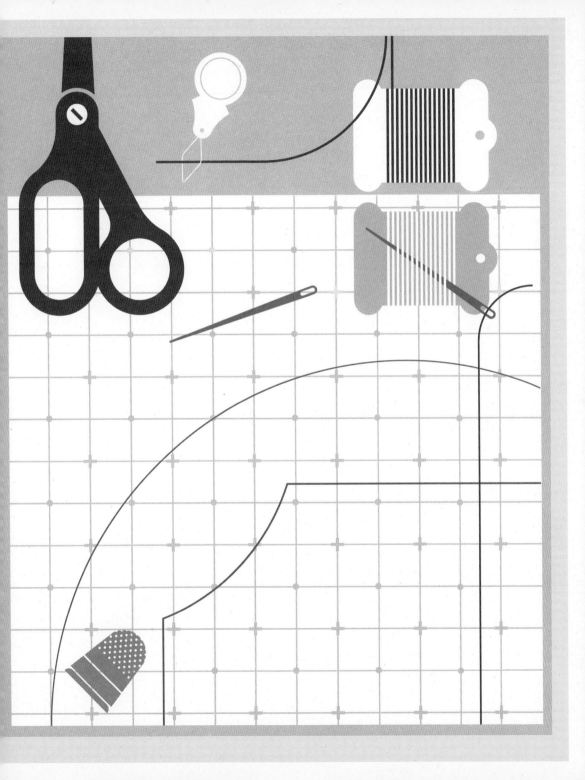

-- Nightie night --

It's best to keep any intervention on delicate fabrics as light as possible, but a few sequins or an offcut of embroidery appliquéd onto a vintage negligee can instantly transform it from pyjama to party. Other ways to adapt such a piece include shortening it to make a camisole or dying pale fabric a darker shade for a more evening feel, and adding piping or trimmings. As an optional extra add feather epaulettes or a short cap sleeve in chiffon, silk or gauze at the shoulder to give more weight.

-- Disarming look --

The special armed forces that are bat-winged tops and dresses can be deployed at the frontline of a stylish wardrobe by upcycling them into tanks. The sleeves join the body somewhere around the waist area so removing them means losing the entire side of the garment and, while it can be a little breezy, it is a flattering style for slim figures. Alternatively, the sides can be rejoined with a simple line of stitching, a double-ended zip or a series of simple ties made from another fabric, strapping, ribbon or elastic. Cut off the sleeves in a vertical line down from the outer edge of the shoulder, and hem or add a fastening accordingly. If leaving the sides open, pair with a bandeau strapless top underneath.

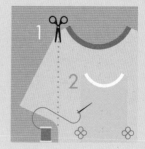

-- Curtain call --

Once an indispensable accessory of suburban living, the lace curtain provided the perfect shield to hide behind and watch the neighbours coming and going. But no longer – as social networking sites have made nosing into other people's lives easier to do online, so the Net Curtain Twitch has fallen out of fashion. The Net Curtain Twirl, on the other hand, is a more modern prospect entirely. The lacy florals found on old net curtains are well suited to dresses, skirts and tops, and a pretty scalloped edge can also be exploited to save the need for hemming. Add a lining in a matching colour to ward off unwanted voyeurs.

People Tree
Sari collection

One of the original and most significant pioneers of fairtrade and environmentally aware fashion on an international scale, People Tree was founded at the start of the 1990s by Safia Minney. Now a globally acknowledged expert on ethical attire operating in the UK and Japan, People Tree strives to bring benefits to people and the planet at every stage of the production and distribution process.

The recycled Sari dresses are, unsurprisingly, made in India. Bright and beautiful cast-off sari silks are adapted into a variety of new dresses – sewn into black organic poplin skirts, embellished with traditional hand embroidery and cinched in and tailored with ties and belts. Offcuts go to make accessories such as bags and quilts.

Gary Harvey
Recycled couture

London-based Gary Harvey was driven to create his label out of creative frustration while working on a campaign shoot. The ex-creative director of Levi Strauss and Dockers Europe found his fix that day from the spontaneous ad hoc construction of a dramatic evening dress and train using 42 pairs of Levi's 501s.

A whimsical way with waste soon developed into a successful signature line in barmy ballgowns. Iconic, everyday garments would be re-contextualized and a close look at any one of his Dior-style "New Look" dresses might reveal 18 Burberry macs or 28 camouflage Army jackets. The pink newspaper dress was made from 30 copies of the *Financial Times*.

Harvey launched his first collection of nine dresses made entirely from second-hand clothing during London Fashion Week in 2007. In 2011 eco-design champion Livia Firth commissioned Harvey to design her dress for the Oscars, where her husband Colin picked up a Best Actor Award. The result, created using 11 vintage dresses all from the era of *The King's Speech*, the winning film, was widely praised as one of the biggest red carpet successes of the year.

Design example
ULTRA
ULTRA 10

Perhaps the ultimate capsule collection, ULTRA 10 is a ten-piece women's wardrobe which, through mixing, matching and adapting, is designed to provide all the outfits a woman would need for an entire year.

Including a coat that turns into both a shirt and a skirt as well as a jacket that converts into a vest, all the outfits are made to order from organic cotton and recycled materials such as jersey, georgette and chiffon. Other possible garments include a backless top, a cropped top, a shirt/dress, a pair of stretch pants and a pair of cotton trousers. In short, everything and then some. The sharply tailored, classic, monochrome pieces work for formal or more casual wear, depending on their combinations, as well as across seasons. The pieces can also be sent back to ULTRA 10 at any time for mending or upcycling, and at the end of the year's wear they can be swapped for a discounted fresh supply.

ULTRA 10 was launched in 2011 by the young Kuala Lumpur-based fashion label ULTRA, whose debut collection only one year before that was produced entirely from sustainable materials such as soy and bamboo, recycled PET and salmon-skin leather.

Design example

Martin Margiela
Deconstructionist fashion

Fashion's deconstructivist movement kicked off with Martin Margiela's very first collection in 1989. After a two-year stint as assistant to Jean Paul Gaultier, Margiela presented a leather butcher's apron reworked into a seductive evening gown and an old tulle dress remodelled into several sharply tailored jackets. Subsequently, Margiela became known for an avant-garde approach and unfinished details. He used traditional lining fabrics as outer layers, left hems and seams rough and trailing, shoulder pads were worn on the outside of clothes, darts were exposed and red Christmas tinsel became a luxurious "fur" coat. Concerned with the natural cycle of objects, Margiela championed remaking and recycling long before the practices were linked with ethical and ecological concerns.

Margiela originally studied at Antwerp's Royal Academy of Fine Arts alongside the group of influential designers that would go on to be known as the Antwerp Six. Due to a shared tendency to rip apart conventional notions of consumerism and reinterpret the fashion rules, he has often been described as though he were a seventh member. Like his contemporaries, Ann Demeulemeester and Dries Van Noten, Margiela would go on to become a key proponent of the intellectual fashion movement during the 1990s, but he has always defiantly stood apart from the pack.

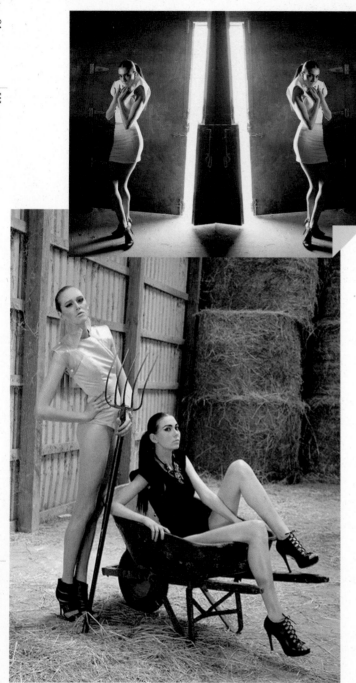

Design example
Angelene Fenuta
Litis

Canadian designer Angelene Fenuta first attracted attention in the fashion media for her thesis collection, Litis, which incorporated industrial plastics. Used in combination with draped satins and stiff tulle, the unconventional textiles lent extreme silhouettes to Fenuta's designs, which distort and reconfigure the body at dramatic angles. Fenuta explains that fashion designers are presented with many restrictions by the human body and traditional fabric types and that the garments in her first collection were meant to illustrate "the experimental evolution of breaking through these barriers, in an attempt to reveal a new sense of innovative freedom in design".

-- Panel decision --

A skirt can be made quickly using two vintage silk neck scarves. Choose two scarves of the same size with matching or coordinating patterns – if there is a border it helps to make sure it is the same on both scarves. Position the scarves back to back and sew up the sides to form a tube. Fold over a top seam and thread through elastic to make a waistband.

-- Till death do us part --

If there's one thing harder than finding The Dress, it's the question of what to do with it after the wedding. Selling it is an option, as is keeping it, in the hope that one day the hypothetical daughter might get married, love it and also fit into it. One alternative way to begin the recycling process, however, is the dress-wreck. This involves restaging the wedding photos with a more carefree feel – rolling in the sand, deep-sea diving, paintballing and so on, all activities promising to maximize the memory mileage of a good dress before retiring it forever. But if a wedding dress is about creating beautiful memories, why not make it work a bit harder and remake it into some new garments for longer-term use instead. Seek advice from a seamstress if necessary: suggestions might include skirts, camisoles and bustiers – or more keepsake items and accessories such as purses and scarves.

-- Knickers with a twist --

Walking under ladders is widely considered bad luck, and that is as true of ladders in tights as it is anywhere else. Where the run can't be caught in time using a dab of clear nail polish or a spritz of hairspray, consider salvaging the good parts as a readymade basis for a new set of lingerie. For knickers, remove the legs, and possibly the waistband, and trim instead using lace or ribbon; add silk or satin panels to create an attractive design. For the top half a section of the widest part of the leg or the waist can make a bandeau-style bra.

STEP-BY-STEP

All in the jeans

While acknowledging that the bond that exists between a person and their favourite pair of jeans can transcend that of almost any other type of garment, and that jeans get better with age and wear, they are still subject to going out of fashion. With the exception maybe of pre-1971 Levi's (which can fetch huge prices as a collectable item: spot them by the uppercase text on the label), a single pair will rarely last forever.

A good pair of jeans can be like a close friend or a loyal dog – reliable come rain or shine, through life's highs and lows, the laughter, the sadness, the crazy nights, the hangovers. But like every relationship, sometimes the day may come when they just don't seem so perfect anymore. Newer, more flattering, fashionable jeans begin to look more attractive...

Facing up to this can be hard. But take comfort in the knowledge that there are hundreds of ways to resuscitate a flagging relationship with an old pair of jeans – starting with the classic denim skirt.

You will need:

- A pair of jeans that fit well around the waist and hips
- Sewing machine
- Thread (either match the top stitching on the jeans or choose a colour that will blend with the denim)
- Scissors
- Tape measure
- Pins
- Chalk pencil

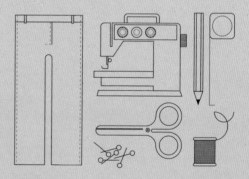

1_ To transform a pair of jeans that you no
longer want to wear day in day out into
a skirt, begin by pressing them well.
Lay them flat on a table and smooth
them out.

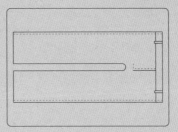

2_ Decide on the length of the skirt you
want to make. This method works
best for a knee-length pencil skirt or
a mini. For a long skirt, however, there
is always the option of adding in panels
later. Measure the length and mark
it using a chalk pencil or pins and then
cut the legs off a few centimetres below
the line to allow for adjustments, wonky
cutting and either fraying or hemming
the edges.

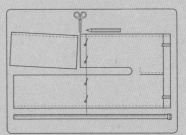

3_ Turn the jeans inside out and remove the inseam stitching to open up to the crotch, resulting in an open garment. Then cut the front up to the zip and the back up to the yolk.

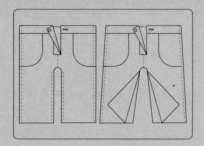

4_ Iron out the seams so that the fabric is as flat as possible and then overlap the front panels to form a straight seam.

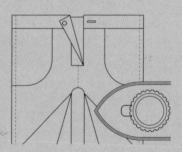

5_ Pin the fabric on the back – depending on how long you are making the skirt this will leave a triangular opening, which you can choose to leave as a split, in the case of a pencil skirt, or fill in with another fabric or leftover fabric from the legs.

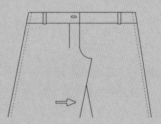

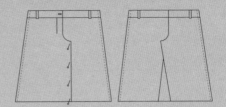

6_ Try it on. Make adjustments and try it on again. This is the crucial stage at which you can eliminate any weird bulges in the fabric and get the perfect length.

7_ When you are happy with the pinned version use the sewing machine to set it in thread.

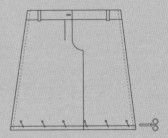

8_ Either pin and hem the bottom at this stage or cut it to the final desired length – frayed edges on denim wear well and are appropriate with this look.

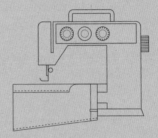

Design example
Airi Isoda
wrk-shp

Being resourceful with materials
can sometimes mean looking
in unlikely places. Airi Isoda, a
fashion designer working with
architect Ryan Upton in the
multi-disciplinary Los Angeles-
based collective wrk-shp,
structured her A/W 2011–12
collection on materials more
commonly found on building
sites and renovation schemes.

   The ready-to-wear line
combined natural fabrics such
as cotton, silk and wool with
accessories and details made
from building materials such
as Tyvek, concrete, wood, metal
and house paint. Clothes, like
buildings, are primarily designed
to protect people from the
outside elements, and in that
way the experimental but still
wearable garments worked to
connect the wearer to the built
environment in a new way.

Design example
Airi Isoda
wrk-shp

Design example

Minna
Wedding collection

Finnish designer Minna Hepburn finds the raw materials used for her eco-luxe clothing label while scouring antique and lace markets on her travels around Europe.

   With no formal fashion training, Hepburn began making clothes as a hobby, before the pieces started finding their way into high-end boutiques. She launched her label, Minna, in 2008. Committed to environmentally friendly production techniques, local manufacturing and zero-waste pattern-cutting, appealing to an audience beyond the ethical consumer has always been a priority.

-- Tight spot --

Feet can have a habit of seeking freedom through the end of a tiny hole in a pair of tights, so when the darning option is looking too darn difficult or dull it is often easier to cut off the entire foot altogether. Over time, as these footless tights amass in number, they can be layered to considerable thickness, eventually passing as a pair of leggings. For the outermost pair take care to choose a design that doesn't feature a visible gusset.

-- Divided loyalties --

Most one-piece garments can be cut down to two — or at the very least one — new piece with some excess matching fabric for accessories. With the help of a pair of scissors and a sewing machine, a dress, for example, will find new life as a skirt and/or a top, and a playsuit as shorts and/or a top. A swimming costume becomes a bikini or tankini and a catsuit can make a leotard or a pair of leggings and a bra. Be mindful of where the fastenings lie before starting, and don't be discouraged if in some cases it is necessary to remove them entirely and replace them. Where buttons are involved, say in a shirtdress, make the cut so the final hem will be just above the line of where the next button would be. Where there is a zip to be navigated either cut just below it, just above it or remove it entirely.

-- Tube planner --

Save a too-small or child-sized T-shirt by turning it into a bandeau — useful on the beach, as an undergarment or a casual summery top. Draw a straight line across the fabric under the arms and cut along it to remove the sleeves and neck, leaving a basic tube shape. Measure and remove a section from the bottom part as well to even out any graphics and adjust the length. Then either leave it as it is or to make a more bikini-style top gather the fabric in the centre and tie using string or a thin piece of ribbon. Finally, bring the strings up and around the neck to create a halterneck.

Design example

From Somewhere
Rescued fabrics

Orsola de Castro and Filippo Ricci established From Somewhere in 1997 as an answer to what they saw to be a pressing need for a genuinely sustainable fashion label that could produce designs in large numbers. Turning its gaze onto the fashion industry itself for an answer, From Somewhere's collections are made using luxury designer pre-consumer waste: rescuing fabrics such as swatches, proofs, production offcuts and end-of-roll textiles from an otherwise tragic fate as landfill or incinerator fuel. Distinctive eclectic colour palettes, simple shapes and original panelling mark out From Somewhere's designs, but its innovative methods mean that every piece is in some way unique. De Castro and Ricci, tireless environmental campaigners beyond the brand as well, also act as consultants to the fashion industry and extended their reach to the high street in 2010 with a collection for the Florence & Fred label for Tesco's supermarket chain, recycling waste from its own supply chain.

MULTIPLE CHOICE

The way we wear
- -

When it comes to transforming a man's shirt into a dress or a skirt, there are more ingenious ways to nip and tuck, lengthen and style according to taste and/or fashion than there are room for in this book. But as is so often the case in design, the simplest solutions are often the most stunning.

With a large shirt, a petite model and a bit of confidence the following ideas can be pulled off with no sewing at all, but for added security and longevity model them, pin them and sew them into place, cutting off any excess fabric where the design seems bulky. To make the designs look even less as though they originated with a shirt, remove the cuffs and the collar before you start.

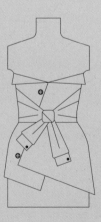

Dress 1_

Take the shirt and wrap it around you, fastening the topmost button you can above the bust. Take the arms of the shirt and bring them to the front, tying them in a knot and arranging the excess into a bow.

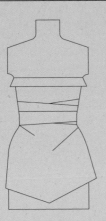

Dress 2_

Wrap the shirt around you again, but back to front so that this time the collar sits above the bust. Cross the sleeves around the front and behind you, tying them in a knot in the small of your back.

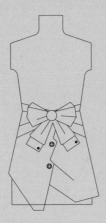

Skirt_

Button the shirt (as far up as will fit) around your waist. Continue buttoning down, but skip every other button hole to create a series of folds. Tie the sleeves together at the front, pulling one through the other to create a half bow.

Top_

Wrap the shirt around you and button over your bust as with dress 1. Skipping a button hole at the top to form a fold, continue buttoning down. Bring the sleeves up, over and around your neck as a halter, tying them in a bow slightly to one side. Add a belt around the waist and adjust the folds until you're happy with them.

Design example

Milch
Everyday upcycling

Milch is an eco-fashion label founded by Cloed Priscilla Baumgartner in Vienna in 1996. Just as the name represents the everyday upcycling processes found in nature – grass to cow to milk, for example – at Milch traditional menswear garments and suiting are radically transmuted into dresses, skirts, blouses and hats for women.

Committed to using high-quality raw materials, the original clothes are sourced locally before being partially dismantled, reconstructed and sewn by hand into the new designs. Elements of their previous incarnation such as collars, waistbands, cuffs and buttons are preserved to provide nostalgic detail in the new pieces, as well as giving a nod to Viennese history and past wearers.

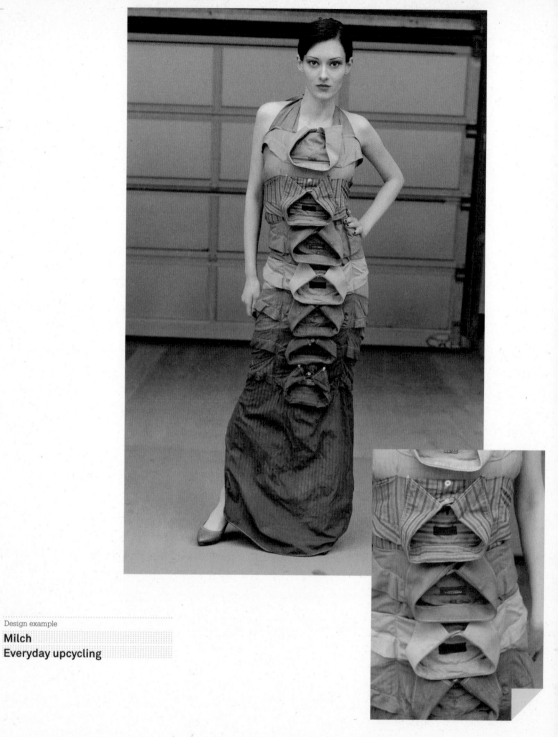

Design example
Milch
Everyday upcycling

Design example

Schmidt Takahashi
Reanimation

At Schmidt Takahashi the history of every piece recycled in the collections is as important as the resulting new garment. In a process they call Reanimation (Wiederbelebungsmassnahmen), the Berlin-based label collects discarded and used clothing in custom-made containers. They then wash, iron and photograph each item, and assign it an identification number. Its previous history, colour, material and style are all meticulously catalogued.

This information is then duly stored on RFID chips and embedded into the new garments – new hybrid configurations of deconstructed old parts. The chips can be easily scanned, read and updated using a smartphone, so the new wearer is able not only to unlock the garment's history, but also to contribute to its ongoing narrative.

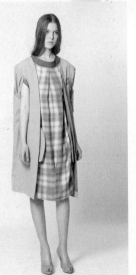

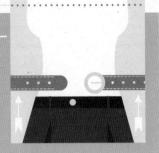

-- Max factor --

Maximize a maxi skirt's usefulness by adapting it into a strapless dress. Pull it up so the waistband sits above the bust, cinching in the waist with a belt. To adjust the length either roll over the top of the now-dress, and/or pull the fabric up over the belt to add more blousiness to the top half. Pair with a blazer over the top or a big shirt, knotted at the waist in place of a belt.

-- diyPad --

Popular in the 1940s, the 1980s and the 2000s, shoulder pads have a powerful past and a sure, sharp future too. A pointed pair of shoulders not only recalibrates the silhouette, whittling down a waist and balancing out the hips, but it is a brilliant way to add edge and attitude to an old blouse or T-shirt, and a quick and easy way to use up scrap fabric at the same time. To start with, measure the shoulders of the garment to be used and cut a circle of scrap fabric of the same diameter. Fill the circle with shredded scraps and fold it in half as if making a Cornish pasty. Pin and sew it around the edges, and then fix the scrap layer in place by stitching a few lines across the pad. Check the two pads have the same consistency and appearance and then fix them into the garment using a couple of discreet stitches at each end of the pad. Voilà – you are ready to make an entrance. Just remember to do it sideways.

-- Wrap genius --

Just as a scarf or a shawl is easily adapted to make a sarong on the beach, the same principle can be used to make a wraparound skirt suitable for any occasion. In place of a knot, gather the fabric and add a buckle to secure the skirt at the side.

<u>STEP-BY-STEP</u>

Dream job

A classic wartime wardrobe staple, the pillowcase skirt has endured since its invention in the 1940s when British women were experts at make do and mend, and Mrs Sew-and-Sew distributed her helpful tips via government-issued pamphlets. Its success comes by virtue of its ingenious simplicity. With readymade side seams and minimal waste, as long as the pillowcase isn't in service at the same time, even the most amateur seamstress can make one in her sleep.

For this design a standard pillowcase will make a skirt to fit sizes 6 to 10 (UK) or 2 to 6 (US). Variations on the same theme include pencil skirts (involving the addition of darts, a waistband and a zip) and pleated versions. Pillowcases themselves obviously vary massively and the result could just as easily feature a retro flower motif as a Spiderman print. White linens lend themselves especially well to tennis skirts.

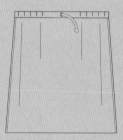

You will need:

- _ A pillowcase
- _ Sewing machine
- _ Thread
- _ Scissors
- _ Tape measure
- _ Pins
- _ Chalk pencil
- _ Safety pin
- _ Elastic (optional)

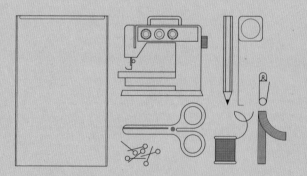

1_ Iron the pillowcase. If the pillowcase has a flap then make sure that it is sitting flat inside before you iron over the top.

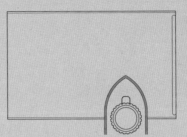

2_ Decide on the length you want the skirt to be and measure from the top of the pillowcase, adding about 10 cm to allow for the waistband and hem. Cut off the bottom (if the pillowcase has a closing flap then cut this top part out as well) which will leave you with a tube of the desired length, plus a strip of extra fabric.

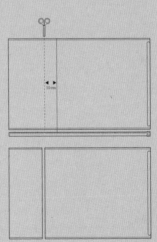

3_ Cut the leftover fabric into thin strips around 2 cm in width – this will be used to make the drawstring later.

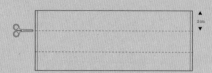

4_ If the pillowcase had a closing flap which you cut out then this end will need to be hemmed. Turn the pillowcase inside out, fold over a neat edge of around 1 cm, press, fold it over again, pin in place and sew.

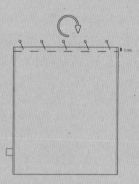

5_ Turn the pillowcase right-side-out. To make the waistband, fold over about 1 cm of fabric at the top of the skirt and press it into place. Then fold over another 2 cm or so, press and pin it into place before sewing close to the bottom edge, forming a neat band for the drawstring or elastic.

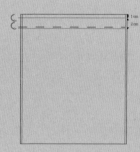

6_ Measure and mark the centre of the
waistband and make a small cut in the
fabric for the drawstring or elastic to
go through. If using elastic, make the
incision discreetly at the side seam.

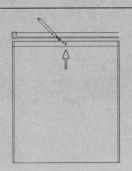

7_ To make the drawstring, take the
offcuts from earlier and sew them
together to make a single, long strip.
Fold this in half lengthways, press
and fold in half again, before pressing
again, pinning and sewing to give you
a long string.

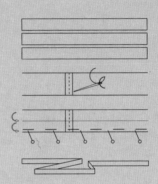

8_ Attach a safety pin to one end of
the drawstring or elastic and feed
it through the slit in the waistband
and gather up the fabric so that it
sits evenly. Remove the safety pin
and finish the ends of the drawstring
with knots or beads or leave loose. For
elastic, secure the ends together before
hiding them and stitching up the
incision by hand.

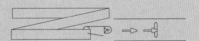

Design example

Christopher Raeburn
Recommissioned textiles

Since graduating from the Royal College of Art in London in 2006, Christopher Raeburn's work in ethical fashion has won him numerous accolades and awards – US *Vogue* even called for its readers to "Remember the 4 Rs: Reduce, Reuse, Recycle, and Raeburn." His label is centred around the reuse of decommissioned military stock, exploiting the functional and waterproof qualities of these textiles as urban outerwear.

The military always have to overproduce their garments so thousands of square metres of military surplus that would otherwise be left to gather dust in storage are used by Raeburn's label, giving it an opportunity to be recommissioned in urban service. Raeburn sources his textiles from all over the world, playing on the different aesthetic and practical qualities of what he finds, whether it is desert camouflage or parachute silk, although usually only in works where he is able to access quantities large enough to make around 100 to 200 of the end garment.

Design example

**Beautiful Soul
Kimono collection**

Beautiful Soul is a luxury British womenswear label established by Nicola Woods in 2008. The Beautiful Soul studio boasts one of the largest archives of vintage Japanese kimonos dating back to the 1940s and it is from this archive that Beautiful Soul's Kimono Collection is created. Retailored into bespoke garments, all designs have an emphasis on multi-functionality and adjustability. The distinctive materials are not only exclusive, but also inspire an emotional urge to treasure and care for the garments over a lifetime.

In addition the "Beautiful Soul London" ready-to-wear collection features strong signature prints and is produced with an environmentally conscious approach through its sourcing of British fabrics and commitment to local, UK-based production.

Beautiful Soul
Kimono collection

Design example
Clements Ribeiro
Half and half

Husband and wife design duo
Suzanne Clements and Inacio
Ribeiro met during their studies
at London's Central Saint Martins
College of Art and Design in 1991
and launched their own label
together two years later.
Soon renowned for their bold
use of pattern and feminine
knits, the pair also have
a less well-known line in
upcycled vintage fashion –
an experiment that began
in 1998 when a collaboration
with embroiderer extraordinaire
Karen Nicol resulted in a
beautiful series of customized
antique cashmere knits.

Other off-catwalk initiatives
in later years have included the
Collage Collection of dresses
and skirts constructed from
vintage couture fabrics and the
Half and Half Project, a limited
range of unique dresses made to
the same pattern using antique
textiles. Half of the dress is of
light, hand-embroidered silks,
the other half of contrasting
heavier weight precious weaves
such as brocade and guipure.

Design example
Antiform
Local fashion systems
When Lizzie Harrison set up her upcycled fashion label Antiform, her mission was not only to make use of the piles of unwanted materials and clothing that she saw were available in her hometown of Leeds, but also to tap the considerable experience in sustainable fashion design, textiles upcycling and local fashion systems in the area.

Antiform was established in 2007 and an ambitious team of local designers, researchers and communicators grew quickly under Harrison's leadership. Working as the in-house brand for partner organization ReMade In Leeds, Antiform also takes a proactive role in local upcycling events, clothes swaps, sewing courses and workshops.

Design example
Piece x Piece
Luxury upcycling
With a view that existing
materials are "a precious
resource" with much untapped
potential, Piece x Piece is
a personal response to the
shocking amount of waste
produced on an ongoing basis by
the fashion industry. Founded by
Elizabeth Brunner in 2008 using
fabric samples to create bespoke
and unique new garments, the
mission of the luxury dress label
is to save fabrics from their more
traditional fate as landfill, while
also creating awareness and
encouraging a new market for
alternatively sourced clothing.

Brunner, who studied interior
architecture and worked
at prestigious design firm
Pentagram before enrolling on
the fashion design program at
the California College of the Arts,
has developed an original and
highly experimental technique
for creating her designs,
each of which is produced in
very limited editions. An involved
and lengthy process, the result
is garments that are trans-
seasonal and timeless
in their design.

MULTIPLE CHOICE

Within the folds

Before the invention of tricky fitted bedsheets, ancient civilizations often fashioned entire wardrobes from the contents of their linen cupboards. With a huge square of fabulous fabric and the support of a good belt, it is possible to make a multitude of dresses, from togas to sarongs, or saris to safari. The art of draping, knotting and belting a large shawl, scarf or similar to best sartorial effect is one worth cultivating. No sewing required.

You will need:

_ A large square shawl
  (140 x 140 cm or larger)
_ A belt
_ Panache

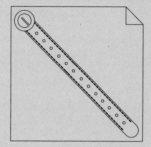

1_ One-strap wonder
   Hold two top corners of the square, wrap the fabric around you, and
   cross the corners over each other, under one arm. Twist the corners
   up and over to form straps, and tie them securely where they meet at
   the top of the shoulder. Belt the dress at the waist.

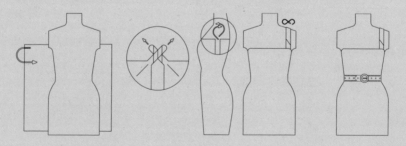

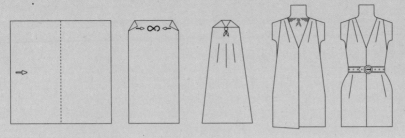

2_ Deep-fronted halterneck

Fold the square in half and tie the two top corners to each other. Step into the dress, putting the knot over your head. Gather the folds together at the front and belt at the waist.

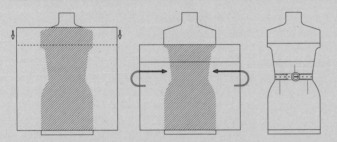

3_ Strapless simple tube dress

Fold over the top of the square to get the desired length for this dress. Otherwise, simply wrap it around you as if it were a towel, secure discreetly at the side under one arm, and belt at the waist.

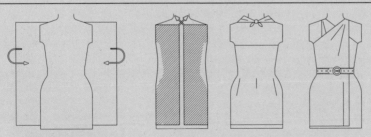

4_ High-neck halterneck

Wrap the fabric around you and pass the two top corners over each other at the front, before taking them behind your neck. Tie in a knot. You can belt this or leave it without.

Design example
Junky Styling
Wardrobe surgery

Junky Styling deconstructs previously worn clothing before mixing it up and rebuilding it into new one-off garments. The brainchild of London-based designers Annika Sanders and Kerry Seager, the idea was to provide a departure from existing upcycling programmes by focusing on flattering designs, quality raw materials and hand-finishing.

Sanders and Seager established successful menswear and womenswear ranges before going on to offer a "wardrobe surgery" at their atelier in East London – a bespoke service where they work with customers' own garments, transforming anything from old band T-shirts to three-piece suits and wedding dresses.

Design example
Rachel Freire
Nippleocalypse

Operating at the more extreme end of the upcycling spectrum, London designer Rachel Freire creates couture from the by-products of the meat and leather industries. In this case, cow nipples.

While the restaurant business has been booming with offal-inspired menus since the turn of the millennium, Freire demonstrates a similar ethos in her nose-to-tail fashion, creating intricate and luxurious pieces from what would otherwise be cast aside. The nipples are collected from the waste in an ethically operated tannery and, while immediately controversial, the designer argues that the materials used in Nippleocalypse are technically the same as those used in any pair of leather shoes or clothing.

Freire created two dresses for Nippleocalypse, making a total of around 3,000 nipple "petals" into bouquets. Bustles, crinolines, necklaces, rings and a crown complete the collection, all creating a truly standout impression.

Design example
Prophetik
Wearable philosophy

Born in Tennessee and raised on a horse farm, Jeff Garner's cowboy attitude (as well as personal mentorships from Calvin Klein and J. Lindeberg) gave him a reverence for the natural environment and instilled in him ambitions to create sustainable fashion. He launched his own fashion and lifestyle brand, Prophetik, in 2002.

With a mission to create awareness around how clothing is produced, dyed and distributed, Garner is always vocal about the source of materials and dyes used in his collections. The all-natural plant and earth-based hues of the A/W 2011–12 collection, for example, included a rich plum colour blended from madder root, rumex (sorrel), logwood and indigo, while the burgundy was a mix of madder root, cochineal, curled dock and gallnut.

Design example

Martina Spetlova
Ethical sourcing

Czech designer Martina Spetlova holds MAs in both fashion and chemistry, which could go some way towards explaining her more experimental use of materials. Mixing Lycra knits with fish leathers, lurex, lambswool and twisted zips, Spetlova's patchwork designs are exquisitely finished and accessorized with un-dyed thin leather belts, thigh garters and scarves.

Spetlova graduated from Central Saint Martins College of Art and Design in London in 2008, having already worked for designers such as Jeremy Scott and John Galliano. Every textile in her collections is ethically sourced and she works frequently with end-of-line fabrics and yarns from European mills which the industry otherwise sees as waste material.

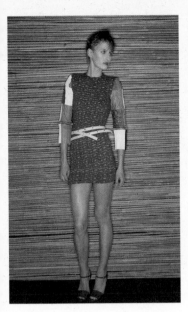

Design example
**Martina Spetlova
Ethical sourcing**

-- Blue jean baby --

Denim cut-offs first emerged as a fashion phenomenon in the early 1970s, with ultra-short jeans hot-pants still known as Daisy Dukes after Catherine Bach's character in *The Dukes of Hazzard*. Now a classic summer look in every length, style and colour, it's always the first and easiest option to get more wear from an old pair of jeans.

-- Great eastern --

The Japanese word "kimono" literally translates as "thing to wear", a phrase that somehow underplays these fantastic full-length traditional robes usually now only worn on special occasions. Although there are not so many occasions, especially in the West, when a kimono may be worn in the conventional manner, as a fabric source for any upcycling project it will provide acres of material as if it has come straight off the roll. Its T-shaped form with its straight edges and long, wide, rectangular sleeves is quite straightforward to dismantle. In Japan, old kimonos are often recycled into handbags and other accessories. The main consideration when adapting a kimono is to be respectful of the pattern and any embroidery and therefore you should find a design that involves minimal cutting and disruption to the often ornate images. Long, simple A-line or wraparound skirts are ideal, as are voluminous simple shift dresses and tops.

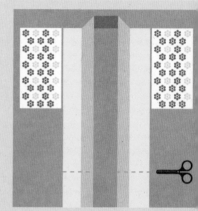

-- Geometry class --

A modest square of fabric – aka the kerchief – has been worn by both men and women for centuries. They are practical, whether worn for extra warmth, or for work, or whipped out to wave off departing lovers, or to wipe away a tear. They are romantic, evocative, nostalgic and fun, and have the ability to lift an otherwise boring outfit. Traditionally, a woman's kerchief is made from cotton, but it may just as easily be linen, wool, silk or lace. It may be patterned or plain, it may have a border or it may not. Worn as a headscarf or round the neck, it can be pinned to the front of a dress or shirt or just as well provide padding for a pocket. To make one, just cut a square of cloth and hem it folding over the smallest amount of fabric you can manage. A triangle can also suffice nicely if you want to cut extra corners...

Design example
Rachael Cassar
Ecouture
Australian "ecouturist" Rachael Cassar launched her eponymous fashion label in 1997 just four months after graduating from the University of Technology, Sydney. She won the prestigious International Mittelmoda Fashion Competition for emerging talent the same year.

One of a new generation of deconstructionists, Cassar's collections are comprised of some 90 per cent recycled materials. The edgy and experimental designs, however, give no hint of this as Cassar, with a strong eye for embellishment and detail, endeavours to show that luxury need not be sacrificed in pursuit of sustainability.

STEP-BY-STEP

Speed date
- - - - - - - - - - - - -

For those last-minute cocktail parties, when your Fairy Godmother has gone
AWOL, a couple of speedy adaptations can magically transform two matching
square silk scarves into an impressive evening dress. No newts, pumpkins or mice
required. And after midnight, this design can be transformed into something else –
a skirt or a luxurious evening cape, for instance.

You will need:

_ 2 matching silk scarves
_ Ribbon or cord
_ Sewing machine
_ Scissors
_ Pins
_ Needle and thread

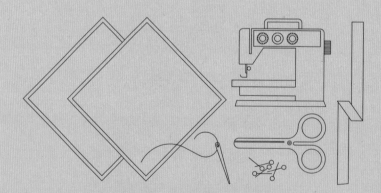

1_ Place the two scarves on top of
each other on a flat surface, right
sides together and with the patterns
matching up.

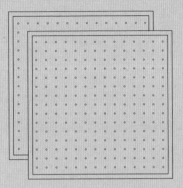

2_Pin and sew one side of the
scarves together.

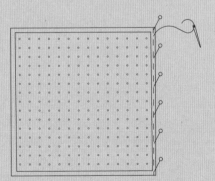

3_ Hold the fabric with the centre seam behind you. Hold the two top corners so that they form two triangles over the bust. Pull the fabric around to the back and mark three points with a pin: A, where the sides of the scarf meet the small of the back; B, where that point meets the centre seam at the base of the back; and C, at the front where you want the scarves to meet (this depends how deep you want the cleavage to sit).

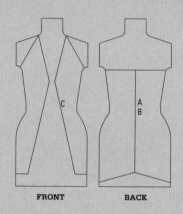

FRONT　　　　**BACK**

4_ Laying the scarves back on the work surface, draw a line from A to B. Pin the scarves together along this line and cut off the excess. Sew a seam along this line.

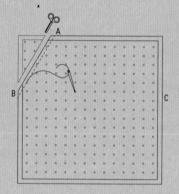

5_ Pin and sew the other side of the scarves together from the bottom of the square to point C. You should now have a tube with one entirely open edge and an open corner. The shorter edge of this corner will be the neckline.

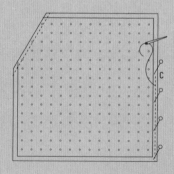

6_ Carefully hem the top edge, with enough room to thread through the ribbon. You can put the cord or ribbon in place before sewing, but be careful not to sew over it while making the hem.

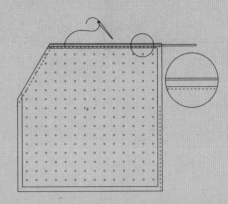

7_ The dress is finished – try it on. You can tie the cord or ribbon around your neck as a halter, and around the dress to change the fit and style.

Design example

Milena Silvano
Earth inspirations

Italian designer and stylist Milena Silvano worked as a designer for Costume National and Jessica Ogden before establishing her own womenswear label in 2001.

Her passion for the natural world and its mysticism led her to follow an environmentally conscious design direction. Her clothes have an earthy femininity, celebrating traditional craft practices while challenging throwaway culture and seasonal trends.

Predominantly working with reclaimed (unused) fabrics and offcuts, Silvano dyes or hand-paints the samples before patchworking them together with organic cotton and non-violent silks to make ethereal dresses, multi-functional shawls and scarves.

Sam Frenzel
Bravade

Mercedes-Benz Fashion Week Berlin 2009 saw the freshly graduated Sam Frenzel pick up the Designer for Tomorrow award. Prestigious at the best of times, with 150 contenders that year alone, it was all the more impressive given that the young German designer had only just shown his debut collection that afternoon.

Frenzel's first collection consisted of sheer blouses, short skirts and leather thigh-high boots – the popularity of which is rarely surprising. But Frenzel's real talent proved to be in his innovative use of materials. Bravade, Frenzel's follow-up collection, contained classic silhouettes and fabrics paired with hard, industrial materials. According to the designer, his process is a bit like baking a cake: "The general ingredients and designs you use are always the same. It's by recombining those ingredients and carefully choosing the right cake tin that you keep the cake delicious."

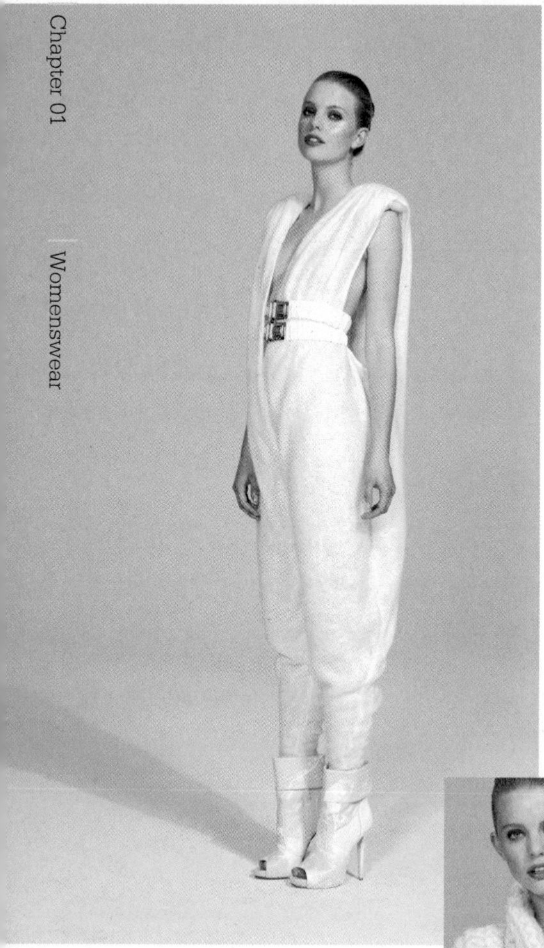

Design example

Sam Frenzel
Bravade

Design example

Goodone
Colour blocking

Goodone was established by Nin Castle and Phoebe Emerson based on the belief that good design ought to provide inspiring and evolving new styles, while still addressing the phenomenal environmental impact of the fashion industry.

The fresh, fashion-forward collections feature upcycled fabrics with sustainable new materials, using a distinctive colour-blocking technique. Winner of several ethical fashion and creative enterprise awards, the label has also created a capsule range for online retailer ASOS and collaborated with Amnesty, Liberty, WWF, Greenpeace, Shelter and No Sweat as part of a project to upcycle old campaign T-shirts.

STEP-BY-STEP

Sleeve it be
- - - - - - - - - - - - - - - -

High-leg foldover leather boots are not something that immediately springs to mind
when thinking of homemade clothes, but with an old leather jacket and a pair of shoes
or ankle boots in a matching colour, it is amazing what you can cobble together.

You will need:

_ Shears (cutting leather with sewing
  scissors will blunt them)
_ Leather jacket (thrift stores do a nice
  line in these)

_ Shoes that match the jacket
_ Stitch unpick
_ Glue
_ Foam (optional)

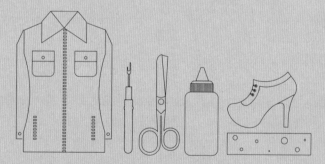

1_ Cut off the sleeves from the leather
   jacket, keeping the lining intact.

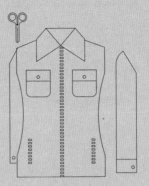

2_ Slide one of the sleeves over your calf
   so that the cuff sits over your ankle, and
   put on the shoe. Adjust the sleeves to
   sit over the tops of the shoe and mark
   the desired length according to how
   much the cover will sit over the heel,
   and how high up the leg it will go.
   Allow for a turn-up of around 2cm
   on the cuff when marking.

2 cm

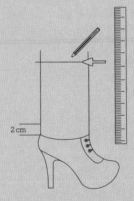

3_ Take off the sleeve, transfer the
markings to the other sleeve, and
cut them both accordingly using the
shears. Now remove the lining.

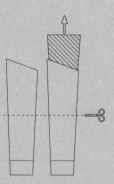

4_ Unpick the seams of the resulting
tubes and trim off the edges to give
a regular oblong or square shape
of leather.

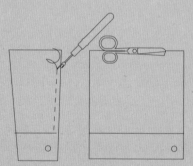

5_ Folding the leather right side in, sew
a new seam vertically up each boot
cover. Use a needle and the appropriate
machine settings specifically for
sewing leather. Flatten the seam
allowance using glue.

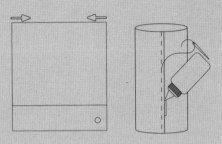

6_ Reinsert the leather tubes into the
old sleeve linings, match up the cuffs
and stitch or glue back into place at
the bottom and top edges, folding the
leather over the lining. For stiff boot
covers rather than slouchy ones,
add a thin foam insert between the
leather and the lining and glue in
place before hemming.

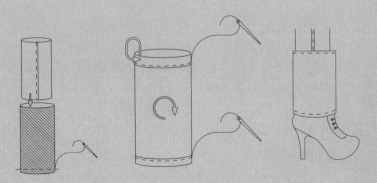

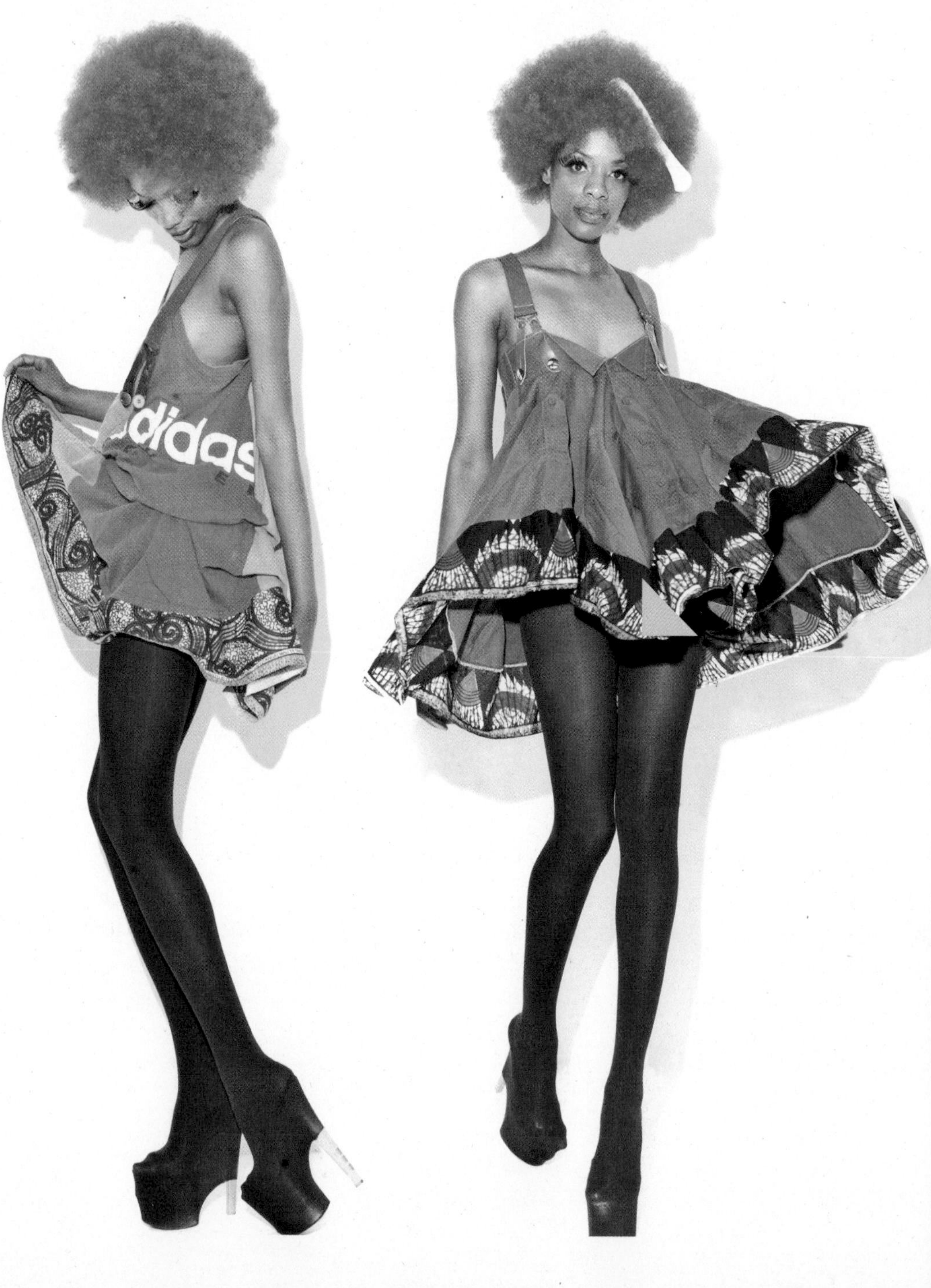

MIA
Africa fashion week

The street markets in Malawi have a raging trade in second-hand clothing, largely imported from Europe and the US. Abundant, cheap and environmentally considerate, accessible apparel is never something to complain about, but the situation has nonetheless created a difficult market for local producers.

Mia Nisbet aims to provide an alternative source of inspiration and carve a new direction for Malawi fashion by fusing recycled fabrics with traditional Malawian textiles. Her award-winning label MIA marries Western styling with rich graphic African prints and is marketed to an international fashion market. Working directly with local producers in Malawi, London-based Nisbet reinvests profits to promote sustainable working practices, providing training and equipment as well as building the infrastructure needed to improve market access.

MENSWEAR

Shorts, cut-offs, shirts, trousers, ties, hats,

jackets, vests, overalls and braces

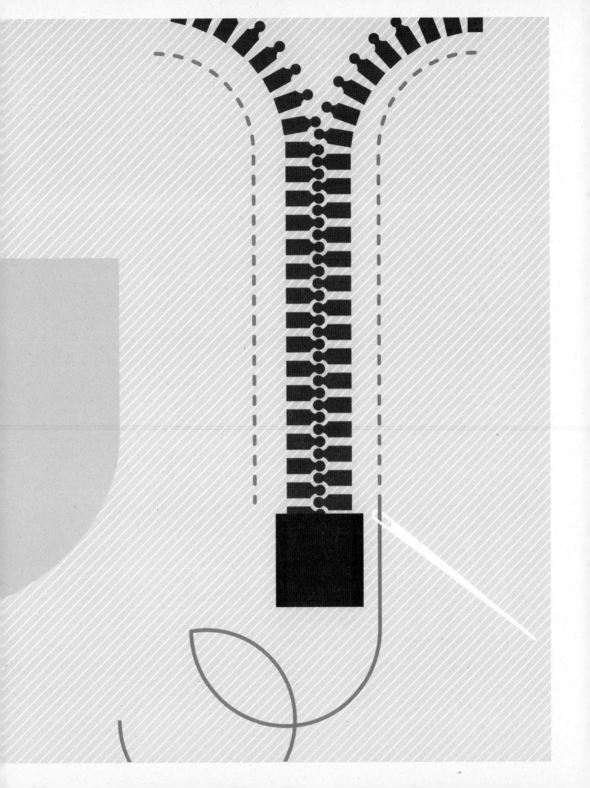

-- Hanky panky --

Beach holidays have been fashionable for centuries, but it was the British man who really raised the sartorial stakes at the seaside when he invented the makeshift hanky hat, which subsequently became a national treasure. First spotted in the 19th century, the knotted hanky hat – made by tying a knot in each corner of a large handkerchief – is not just a useful head protector on a hot day, but it is also a British icon. Best paired with rolled-up corduroys for a quick paddle in a cold sea or worn in the garden while eating a slightly soggy sandwich and drinking a cup of milky tea.

-- Patch testing --

Elbow patches were historically employed in order to prolong the life of a jacket or coat, along with a leather trim around the cuffs. Although largely forgotten in an era of fast fashion, the fact remains that these two straightforward measures can add another ten years onto a garment's service. And whether the motivation is a precautionary measure, a repair job or purely decorative, the end look is still one that suggests practicality, foresight and efficiency. To make your own, find a piece of scrap fabric, leather or suede for the patch – it is best to use something that has the same stretch as that of the garment. Measure and mark each sleeve where you want the patches to go, and cut two elongated ovular patches from your chosen scraps or offcuts. Sew them to the sleeve using a close and wide zigzag stitch around the outer edge.

-- Sweat and match --

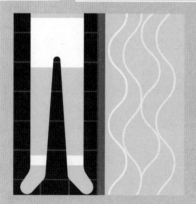

So you made the move to sunny California and your cross-country skiing days are over, but it doesn't mean that those thermals need go to waste. Remove the legs from a pair of long johns for an altogether airier pair of pants and cut down that long-sleeved T to a vest. The foot cuffs will double up as wristbands and the leftover leg parts can be fashioned as a matching sweatband – a whole ensemble ready to be sported poolside at your new pad, while rocking to the beat of a young, earth-loving generation and practising dynamic yoga moves on the roof deck.

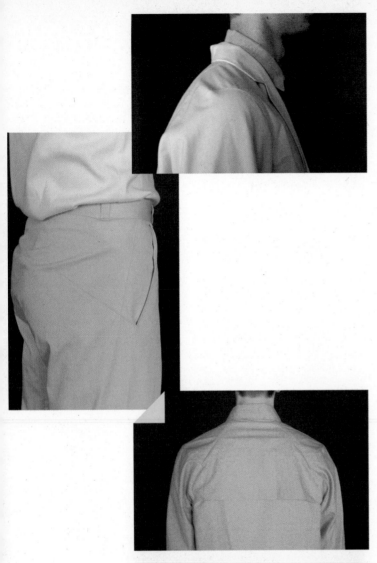

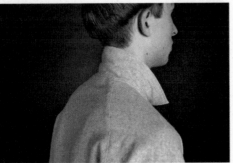

Design example
David Telfer
Minimal seam construction

David Telfer first became interested in the idea of minimal seam construction in 2008 while studying fashion at the University of Brighton. He set himself the challenge of creating an outfit of garments made with just four seams each – the premise being that with fewer seams the garment can be manufactured more efficiently. While the idea would still need work, given its limitations in fabric use, design and fit, Telfer's research proved a jumping-off point for new approaches to fashion production.

In a follow-up project, Telfer delved into the similarly under-explored world of one-piece construction, creating a series of garments each made of a single length of fabric.

Telfer was invited by Timo Rissanen and Holly McQuillan to take part in the exhibition 'Yield: Making Fashion Without Making Waste' in New Zealand. He used the opportunity to develop a minimal seam, one-piece, zero-waste duffle coat made out of heavy wool.

Design example

Schmidt Takahashi
Remaking history

A partnership between Eugenie
Schmidt and Mariko Takahashi,
the Berlin-based label has
a clear Japanese aesthetic.
The garment remixes are
both distinctive and highly
unconventional – a men's
checkered jacket could be cut
with a woman's fur coat, for
example, or a light silk shirt
might evolve into a summer
dress before being belted with
a heavy jersey knit.

-- Inside job --

Subtly customize a leather jacket, a bag or a pair of boots using studs, paint, sheepskin or fur on the lining. Colours and textures on trimmings and interior elements will add a fresh punk edge to an otherwise classic look without being too overt. Furnish a pair of old military boots with extra hardware low on the lacing (around ankle level). Turn down the back, sides and the tongue and then add rows of studs to the down-turned sections.

-- Working wardrobe --

Known on mainland Europe as dungarees, in the US as overalls and in the UK as a boilersuit, wherever you are in the world this workwear classic is cheap, easy to adapt, upcycle and customize, if only because there is so much to work with. Most, too, can be made to be twice as useful by detaching the trousers from the top. The boilersuit can be transformed into a jacket, while by removing the top and adding a belt and turn-ups a great pair of jeans or workwear pants can be made.

-- Tied down --

Tie making is a time-honoured and complex craft, requiring a flawless length of heavy silk cut cleanly on the bias and a familiarity with a multitude of complex parts – the blade, the tail, the neck, the anchor and the processes involved in tipping, slipping and tucking them all just so. Not something to attempt at home, then, nor, with all that bias cutting, is it especially environmentally efficient. There is, of course, the option to break ties with the tie and improvise. And the contemporary cravat provides a far broader church of neckwear by any stretch of raw textile and imagination.

In the early 1800s, the tying of a neck scarf was an artform requiring meticulous precision and a self-respecting gentleman might change his cravat as many as three times a day to suit different activities and occasions. Styles for knotting – of varying degrees of ridiculousness – can be seen in the *Neckclothitania*, a satirical guide published in September 1818, when the craze for cravats had reached elaborate proportions.

Design example

Dr Noki
NOKI

Dr Noki is an activist for environmental and ethical fashion like no other. With a high-energy, highly subversive, counter-culture approach to upcycling and ad hoc alteration, his trademark piece is the Noki-SOB (Suffocation Of Branding) mask, which – along with the rest of his creations – can be read as an assault on homogenous, mass-produced fashion.

Taking his inspiration from anywhere from Shakespeare to deadstock denim, Dr Noki uses vintage clothing, unwanted garments, rags and offcuts to make his one-of-a-kind pieces. Eschewing traditional pattern-cutting methods, instead he chops, dissects and twists the textiles, re-structuring and splicing them together. Based in London, the Edinburgh School of Art trained designer worked with Helen Storey, Whitaker Malem and Owen Gastor before setting up his own label – the NHS or "Noki's House of Sustainability".

STEP-BY-STEP
_____

Brace yourself

Suspenders or braces were originally invented to hitch up the newly fashionable high-waisted trousers of the early 1800s, a style that didn't really work with a belt. Traditionally perceived as underwear, over the years they've gradually emerged as a garment type with a personality all of their own, pinging proudly on the chests of stockbrokers and punks, advertising execs and skinheads. There are a few different ways to make them, all of them easy. The most comfortable kind have straps that are only elasticated at the attachment ends, although fully elastic straps (as shown here) are also an option. Clips can be substituted for buttons, giving the suspenders more versatility as they don't have to be worn with the dedicated trousers. For this design you can repurpose ties, luggage straps, belts, upholstery webbing or salvaged elastic from other garments or offcuts of any sturdy fabric.

You will need:

_ 6 buttons
_ Wide elastic (around 1 m, or shorter, lengths sewn onto the ends of your chosen straps)
_ Leather (cut pieces from any unwanted or thrift-store item)
_ Stanley knife
_ Trousers
_ Needle and thread

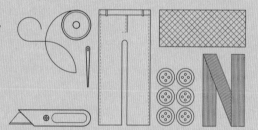

1_ Cut the leather pieces from the thrift-store handbag or whatever you've found for this purpose. You will need one diamond shape (about 3 cm on each side) and three strips around 9 to 10 cm in length for the yoke pieces.

2_ Measure, mark and cut button holes into each end of the three leather yoke pieces using a stanley knife, and check that the buttons will fit through each one.

3_ Fold the middle section of the yoke pieces in half lengthways and stitch in place.

4_ Measure and cut the elastic/straps to form three pieces – two longer pieces that will run from the front of the trousers to the middle of the back between the shoulder blades, where they will meet the third piece and form a Y shape. This last piece will be much shorter and run to the centre of the trousers at the back.

1_

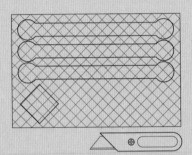

2_

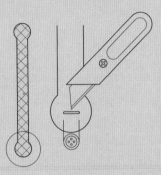

3_

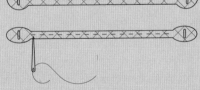

4_

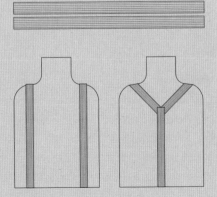

5_ Hem one end of each of the elastic pieces around the centre of the leather yoke pieces. Make sure the stitching is strong here by running a couple of lines back and forth, as this is where most of the stress will be when the suspenders are worn. The leather should be encased snugly, but should still be able to move a little.

6_ Sew the elastic straps together to form a Y shape with the two long elastics at a 45 degree angle to each other. Make sure the seams are all facing the same way. Again, reinforce the stitches by going over them a few times.

7_ Position the leather diamond shape where the elastics meet to cover the join, and top stitch around the edges.

8_ To add the buttons to the trousers measure carefully against the suspenders before you start, drawing an imaginary line up the centre of the front of each leg and position the buttons either side of this line. At the back of the trousers the buttons should go either side of the centre point of the waistband. The buttons can go on the inside or outside of the trousers, as preferred.

5_

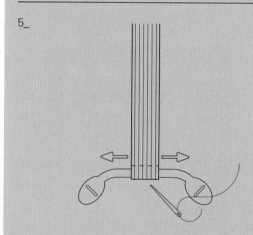

6_

7_

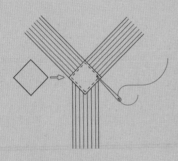

8_

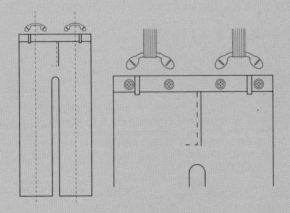

Timo Rissanen
Yield

When Timo Rissanen's grandmother got married in Finland during the Second World War, she received a pair of sheets as part of her dowry. Some years later, heavily repaired to preserve them through times of rationing and shortages, Rissanen would acquire them himself. But they were fit for only one thing.

As part of his role as Assistant Professor of Fashion Design and Sustainability at Parsons The New School for Design, New York, one of Rissanen's responsibilities included finding new ways to incorporate sustainability into the four degree programs in the School of Fashion. He had been exploring the subject for some time (he had taught fashion design at the University of Technology, Sydney, for seven years and had run Usvsu, his own menswear label in Sydney) and his PhD project had been entitled "Fashion Creation Without Fabric Waste Creation" and involved a collection of menswear. In 2011, he co-curated 'Yield: Making Fashion Without Making Waste', a travelling exhibition of zero-waste pattern-cutting. Rissanen's grandmother's sheets were a perfect potential exhibit for the show and were swiftly remade – with no offcuts – into a pair of pyjamas.

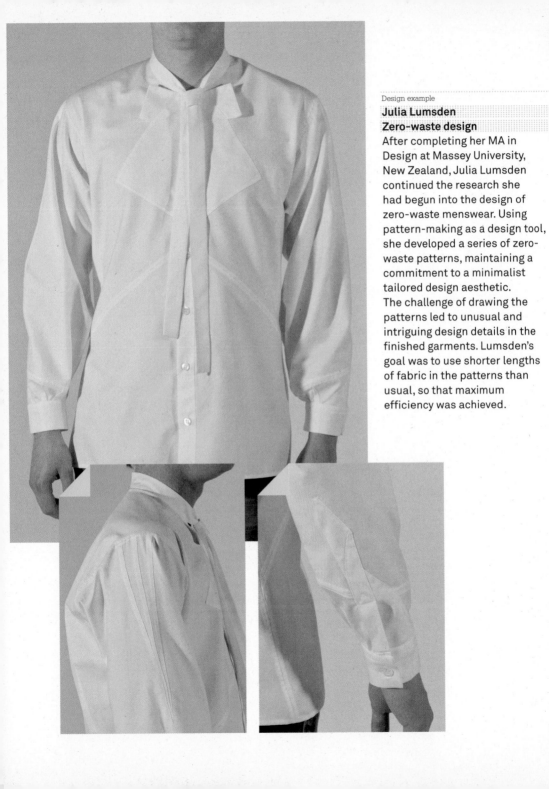

Design example

Julia Lumsden
Zero-waste design

After completing her MA in Design at Massey University, New Zealand, Julia Lumsden continued the research she had begun into the design of zero-waste menswear. Using pattern-making as a design tool, she developed a series of zero-waste patterns, maintaining a commitment to a minimalist tailored design aesthetic.

The challenge of drawing the patterns led to unusual and intriguing design details in the finished garments. Lumsden's goal was to use shorter lengths of fabric in the patterns than usual, so that maximum efficiency was achieved.

STEP-BY-STEP

Turning a collar on a shirt

Men's shirts tend to show wear first on the collar where it rubs on the nape of the neck. The traditional and easiest way to fix this is to turn the collar. Alternatively, or if you run out of steam while pressing and can't get the collar looking pristine enough, leave it off entirely and just stitch up the opening for an instantly revitalized "grandad" or "mandarin" shirt.

You will need:

- Shirt
- Stitch unpick
- Iron
- Needle and thread or sewing machine

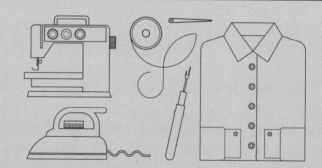

1_ First check that the collar in question is not reinforced by plastic strips on the underside, and also that the underside is itself in good enough condition to face the world.

2_ Unpick the collar carefully to separate it from the shirt using a stitch unpick, removing stray threads along the way.

3_ Then take the collar piece and press it on both sides until the fabric lies as smoothly as possible.

4_ Reposition it into the neck of the shirt with the worn side facing down, and stitch it carefully back into place using the machine, or by hand, with a careful overhand stitch on both sides to keep the stitches as invisible as possible.

1_

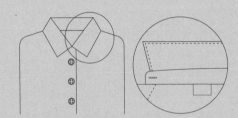

2_

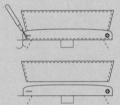

3_

4_

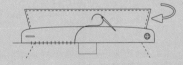

Design example
Junky Styling
Mutant couture
Described by the *New Yorker*
as "an eccentrically chic line of
mutant couture", Junky Styling is
the brainchild of London-based
designers Annika Sanders and
Kerry Seager. The pair, who
had no formal training as
designers, set up their workshop
in 1997, having been inspired
by recycling schemes and
resourcefulness they had seen
on their travels to San Francisco,
Vietnam and Tokyo. Junky Styling
deconstructs previously worn
clothing before mixing it up and
rebuilding it into new, one-off
garments (see also pages 64–65).

Design example
Christopher Raeburn
Army surplus
Christopher Raeburn's clothes
invariably have a few war
tales built in – whether it is
a windcheater made from
parachute fabric or a 1950s
Swiss military raincoat
remodelled into an updated Pac-
Away mac. Sourcing his textiles
from all over the world, the
London-based designer adapts
his collections to play on the
different aesthetic and practical
qualities of what he finds – be it
desert camouflage deadstock or
otherwise. The key is in finding
fabrics in quantities large
enough to make around 100–200
of each garment. Attention to
design and detail is paramount
to Raeburn, who has also worked
on a project with ethical fashion
organization Worn Again to make
a series of bags from Virgin
Atlantic uniforms.

Design example
Alabama Chanin
Studio style DIY
Natalie Chanin's couture
line, which uses upcycled
and repurposed materials in
combination with 100% organic
cotton, is made by teams of
local artisans skilled in the
traditional quilting and stitching
techniques of the region. With
a cult following across the US,
the label grew steadily from its
inception in 2006 into a popular
lifestyle brand focusing on slow
design and sustainability.

Chanin established the
label after spending ten years
working as a stylist and costume
maker for film and photography
in Europe.

Based on the idea that good
design should be a part of
everyday living, Chanin's aim is
to give modern context to these
old methods, ensuring that
they will continue to be passed
down through the generations.
This philosophy is evident in
the workshops where it is not
unusual to find stitchers in their
twenties working alongside
those in their seventies, and
the signature of the artisan who
hand-stitched every seam can
be found on each piece.

-- Take arms --

Give an old shirt a new look by shortening the sleeves or taking them off altogether. For a casual result that works especially well with denim or plaid/check shirts, hems can be left raw or given a slim turn-up for a more polished presentation. Other easy adaptations include the addition of a contrasting flap to a breast pocket or piping along the seams.

-- Sail of the century --

Surplus or redundant sailcloth and tarpaulin are ideal for upcycling into outerwear such as jackets and rain ponchos where the textile's waterproof, windproof and otherwise thoroughly rugged properties can be most effectively exploited. Any existing reinforced grommets can also come in useful – add more if necessary and thread a rope through to provide a drawstring closure for a bag.

-- Knees up --

In menswear, shorts are always casual. Logic dictates few formal or professional advantages from a show of knees, nobbly or not. However, that is not to say that a long-serving pair of summer-suit trousers shouldn't relax into a sunny retirement with a new attitude and a new purpose. Measure, mark and cut the legs to a few inches longer than the desired length and hem accordingly – allowing also for a turn-up. The recommended hem length is a question of aesthetics, but just grazing the top of the knee is fairly failsafe if unsure, while the narrower the trouser leg is to begin with, the shorter the shorts can be.

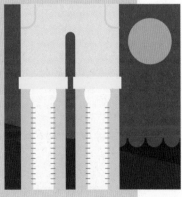

Design example
Prophetik
Sartorial storytelling
Jeff Garner's Prophetik label is
sustainable fashion, Southern-
style. The Tennessee-born
designer often nostalgically
references the bygone days of
his hometown in his collections
in which organic materials and
natural dyes feature strongly.

Garner is also keen to
challenge the design practice
known in fashion as "built-
in obsolescence". Poignant
upcycling projects drive
this home – such as when
for A/W 2011–12 he sent his
grandmother's 100-year-old
quilt down the catwalk newly
retailored into a long quilted
jacket. Another jacket was
reportedly crafted from the
quilted bedspread that Garner
used as a child.

-- Trail blazer --

To be able to wear a suit jacket comfortably as a blazer – i.e., with non-matching trousers – the jacket has to be demonstrably, properly divorced from its other half. A trial separation is simply not convincing, made less so by the inevitable, even if only occasional, reunion further down the line. There are various steps that can be taken to launch an old jacket into a fabulous new single life, however, starting with a subtle makeover: add new buttons, elbow patches or trimmings to show new-found charisma and independence.

-- Utility chic --

Perhaps the most practical item in any man's wardrobe, and yet the most frequently overlooked today, is the neckerchief. A less formal neck tie than the wealthy man's cravat, the working man of yesteryear wore his daily, as did (and still do) most superheroes, action heroes, explorers, adventurers, artists and philosophers, all of whom will testify that a simple cotton square of fabric can be more useful than a Swiss Army knife in an emergency. And not just those of the sartorial sort: because what may be a neckerchief one moment might be a sling the next. It could be a napkin, a washcloth, a sweatband, a bandage, a gag and a souvenir over the course of one (quite exciting) day. Best of all, is that this multi-functional item of wonder-wear can be made from almost any scraps of a suitable medium-weight material (an old cotton shirtsleeve will do nicely) folded or cut into a triangle and hemmed around the edges. Wear it either under or over the shirt collar, tied in a knot at the front.

-- Cut-off point--

As a menswear option, denim cut-off shorts have suffered some controversy over the years. However, practicality will prevail and in an about-turn of which the Dukes of Hazzard would have been proud, they have become some of the chicest menswear on the Med. The key (as for all shorts) is in a tanned calf, the appropriate shoe, and getting the right length, which for most people lands just above the knee. Iron, measure and mark the jeans before cutting, allowing for turn-ups and some room for adjustment.

EVERYONE

Jeans, trousers, T-shirts, shorts, gilets, vests,
tracksuits, socks, ponchos and slippers

STEP-BY-STEP

Time for T

Old T-shirts are the lazy remaker's best friend, if only because they afford a cheap place to start and, like denim, do not necessarily require sewing to finish off the edges. When cotton jersey is cut along the grain it becomes a magical self-hemming fabric: all you need to do is to stretch the edge slightly before releasing it again, making the edges furl under. The end result is pleasingly rock and roll, and even more pleasingly comfortable. Here are some tips for ten classic cuts:

You will need:

_ An old T-shirt
_ Thread
_ Scissors
_ Buttons/jewelry
_ Old shirt

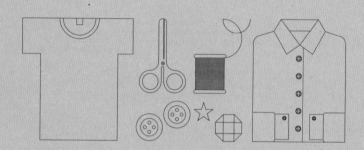

1_ Cut the hems off the arms to change the length to a shorter sleeve, a cap sleeve or no sleeve at all for a vest.

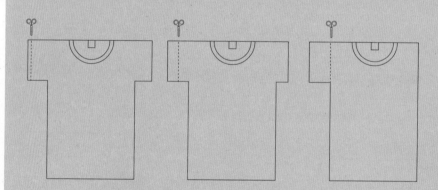

2_ Cut the collar off the neckline – to avoid sewing a new one, go for a boatneck – cut as straight as possible across the fabric under the hem.

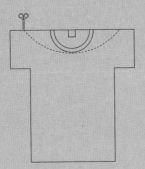

3_ Cut the hem off the bottom to change the length to match the finish of the new sleeves and neckline and/or transform it into a crop top for wearing with high-waisted bottoms or rock-hard six-pack abs.

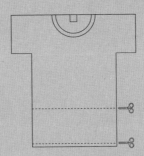

4_ If the T-shirt is tight enough, cut the top half off entirely to create a boob tube. Make a long string with the offcuts and use this to pinch in the centre and form a bikini top with or without a halterneck.

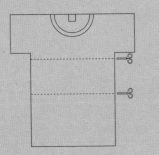
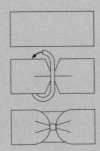

5_ Go cowboy and cut fringes into the sleeves or, for a real trailer trash look, slash horizontal slits into the body.

6_ Cut a shaped neckline, either a deeper round, a V or a low back. Bear in mind that the edges will not furl with some shapes, so a hem may be required to give the result more longevity and neatness.

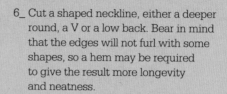

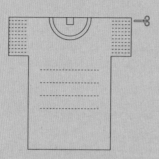

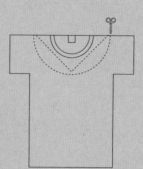

7_ To turn an old T into a strap vest first cut off the sleeves, then cut the neckline into a square, leaving two wide bands. Cut the shoulder seam out and cut the bands into three sections. Plait these into four straps and join the straps together again at the shoulders using a strip of leftover T-shirt fabric to bind them.

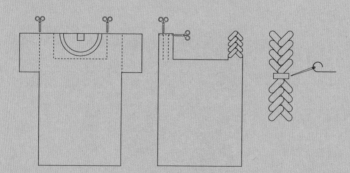

8_ Alternatively, instead of braiding the straps, wind a thick thread around the bands to cover them, as though making a hair wrap. To make sure it will be secure, start by stitching the thread into the T-shirt and then cover the stitches with the wound thread.

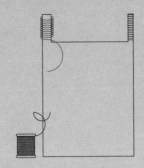

9_ Over-enthusiastic coffee drinking can knock years off the lifetime of a great white T, but where stains can't always be patched over or dyed, they can usually be printed over or written out with a permanent marker and a good slogan or drawing. One classic idea for the latter is to outline trompe-l'oeil buttons or jewelry onto the front.

10_Or you can renovate the T instead with the real thing and sew the collar, a strip of buttons and sleeve cuffs from an old shirt onto a T to smarten it up instantly without compromising the comfort factor. This works best where the garments being used are the same colour.

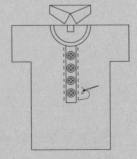

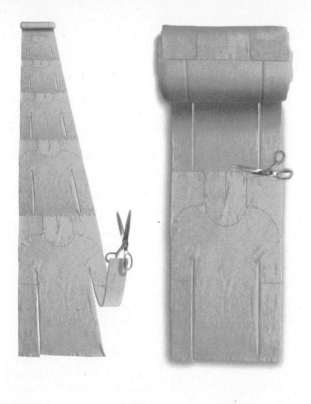

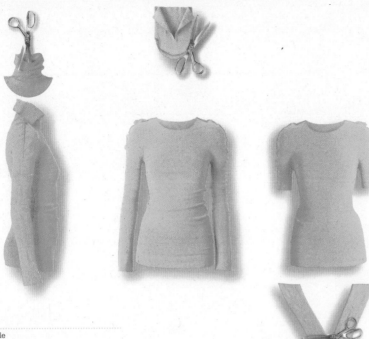

Design example

Issey Miyake
A-POC

Issey Miyake's technology-driven, intellectual approach to clothing design has been shaking fashion's foundations since the 1970s. One of his earliest and most radical concepts, first presented as "A Piece Of Cloth" in 1976, saw the invention of "two-dimensional clothing", a conceptual collection in which the models were sent down the catwalk wrapped in a single length of fabric. Making much use of "ma", a core pillar of Japanese aesthetics that roughly translates as "space", this universal approach to dressing was controversial in that it transcended the physical differences of gender, age or weight, instead creating abstract, asymmetric and sculptural shapes around the body.

In 1999 Miyake developed the concept further with A-POC, an invention devised with the help of Dai Fujiwara, a textile engineer and designer who would later go on to become the label's creative director. Essentially a range of "tubular knitwear" – produced in huge rolls on specially adapted knitting machines – the edges of A-POC garments are built in to the fray-free fabric, and so have no machine-sewn seams. Instead they can be cut by the customer into endless variations – length, shape or style – while one size of the stretch knit flatteringly fits all.

Design example
Julia Crew
Upcycled fabric bags

On completing her MA at the London College of Fashion, Julia Crew opened a studio and shop in London's East End in 2010 with three of her fellow graduates. A collaborative work space, Here Today Here Tomorrow is where Crew's own brand began to take shape. Using materials, including pre-consumer waste (end-of-line upholstery fabrics and off-cuts) and salvaged post-consumer items such as second-hand leather jackets and belts, Crew's approach to the designing process does not stop at responsible sourcing or durable design, but involves what she describes as "customer lifestyle engagement".

Keen to engage with people on a level above and beyond passive consumerism, Crew makes durable design, robust fabrics and constructions, and timeless aesthetics integral to her sustainable approach, while also encouraging her customers to buy one product – rather than many. In order to do this, the bags need to be longlasting in terms of construction, fashion and usefulness. Many of her pieces are created with cyclists in mind, so the products are aligned with a healthy and low-carbon lifestyle too.

Elvis & Kresse
Fire-hose accessories

Tea and coffee sacks, air traffic control flight strips, shoeboxes, opticians' lens boxes, end-of-line labels, old newspapers, used jiffy bags and teabag paper are just some of the raw materials used by Elvis & Kresse to make their bags, belts and accessories.

But it was when the London-based duo met the local Fire Brigade that they really struck gold – in an instant the designers fell in love with their old hoses and saw potential for their first range of products. Despite a noble career fighting fires and saving lives, decommissioned hoses are simply relegated to landfill, but Elvis & Kress wanted to reprocess what they saw as a truly remarkable and sustainable textile. Once clean of the soot, grease and dirt of some 25 years of service, the hoses are cut and re-engineered into a red, hot series of durable and waterproof bags and wallets. In order to thank Britain's fire brigades, Elvis & Kresse feed back half of their profits to the Fire Fighters Charity.

STEP-BY-STEP

Time to dye

From mulberries to molluscs, coffee to camomile, bark to bugs, people have been chopping, powdering and boiling the contents of their local environment to make dyes for as long as they've been wearing clothes at all. A rainbow of beautiful colours can be produced as well as an understated palette of sophisticated neutral shades. The best way to get the right hue for you is to experiment.

You will need:

- Plant material for making the dye – flowers should be in full bloom, berries should be ripe and nuts mature
- Fabric to be dyed. Natural materials such as muslin, silk, cotton and wool work best, and keep in mind the original colour of the fabric when considering the final outcome

- Water
- A huge saucepan
- Large pot
- Salt (for berry dyes)
- Vinegar (for plant dyes)
- Rubber gloves
- Knife
- Sieve

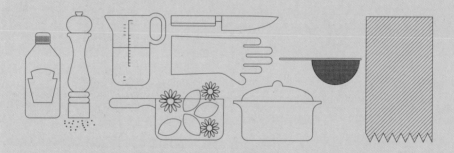

1_ Chop the plant material into very small pieces and place in a pot. The more plant material you have, the stronger the colour will be. Add twice the amount of water as you have plant material. Bring to the boil and then simmer for around an hour. Strain the coloured liquid into a large pot and throw away the remaining gunk.

2_ The fabric to be coloured needs to be soaked in a fixative before the dying process. Simmer the fabric in a solution of 1/2 cup of salt to 8 cups of water or 1 cup of vinegar to 4 cups of water, for about an hour.

3_ Strain off the remaining fixative and add the dye solution to the wet fabric in the saucepan. Simmer until the desired colour is achieved, bearing in mind that when the fabric dries the colour will be lighter.

4_ Rinse the material with cold water and squeeze out the excess. Repeat the rinsing process until the water runs clear.

5_ When laundering the dyed fabric remember to wash it in cold water and separately from other items. The colour may fade slightly over time.

1_

2_

3_

4_

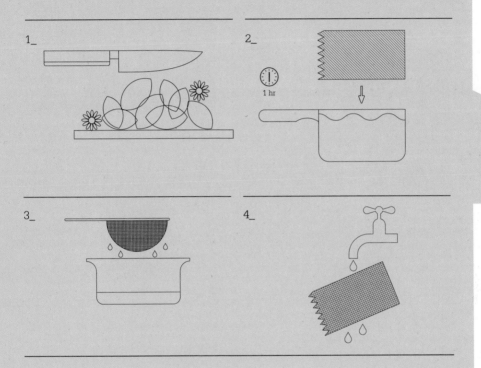

5_

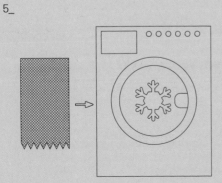

-- Exercise control --

Cut down the arms and legs of an old tracksuit for a fresh set of summer workout wear. Although the fabric shouldn't need hemming, it will look better and last longer if you do. To keep the existing elasticated cuffs on a pair of sweatpants, while still shortening them, cut out a section from the calf and reattach the cuff just below the knee – a pair of sweat-capri-pants. Shortening the legs into running shorts is easier still; snip a tiny indent into the outer-edge seam for a flattering look.

-- Signal flare --

Bell-bottomed trousers, once the preserve of 19th-century sailors and seamen, have – largely thanks to their flattering effect on the wearer's behind – enjoyed as much popularity as they have ridicule over the years. In their rich and fun-filled fashion history their position has always been unequivocal: very much in or very much out. One thing is for sure, there are no halfway measures with flares (that, afterall, would be a bootleg). Best suited to jeans as a remaking project, it's easy to give a straightlegged old pair a new flare by unstitching the outer leg seam to the knee and sewing in a triangular panel of scrap denim or – for a more 1970s carwash look – another, more colourful fabric such as flowery terry cloth will do nicely.

-- Shower power --

The bath cap, a humble but useful protector-of-dry-hair, is easy to fashion from a redundant shower curtain or – better yet – homemade plastic bag fabric (see pages 150–151). To make a version with a pretty fabric cover, layer the plastic circle with another one the same size in cotton and sew around the edges. Thread elastic through the turnover seam.

-- Leg go --

Chop the legs off a pair of leggings or long johns and what you are left with is a sturdy pair of pants and useful tubes that can be cut down to size and repurposed as sleeves on another garment. Unlike prosthetic surgeons, remakers with this cut-and-paste approach to clothing will often find that limbs are widely interchangeable.

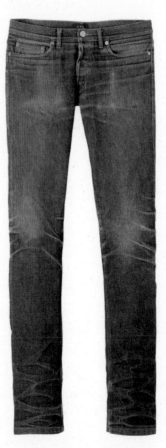

Design example

A.P.C.
Butler jeans

During the 19th century any English aristocrat who wanted to avoid looking "nouveau riche" would have his butler wear a freshly purchased item of clothing for a day or two before stepping out in it themselves. While the call for such a service disappeared along with the exit of Jeeves and the rest of the domestic staff over the years, the fact remains that some types of clothing will always look better when they've seen a little action. Jeans are a case in point – although not everyone holds the same view.

On realizing that his customers fell into two distinct groups, Jean Touitou, founder of French label A.P.C. (Atelier de Production et de Création), had an idea. For those who only want to wear a pair of jeans when they are pristine, he offers a service whereby they can be returned and exchanged for a new pair at cost once they've seen some wear and tear. A.P.C. then takes these old jeans, washes, mends and marks them with the initials of the person who wore them, before reselling them as part of a dedicated line: Butler Jeans.

MULTIPLE CHOICE

Thread betting

There are many unexpected household items that can provide material for a good homespun yarn. Eager weavers, knitting kings and crochet queens can take their crafts to new extremes using newspaper, old T-shirts, cassette tape and plastic bags. And what doesn't knit into a nice bobble hat will surely make a great shoelace at the very least.

You will need:

_ Plastic bags, T-shirts or a garment to be unravelled (for this purpose imagine a sweater)

_ Scissors

_ Iron

_ A niddy-noddy (make one by hammering long nails 90 cm apart in a plank of wood) to wind the wool onto (or you can also wind it into balls)

_ Baking parchment

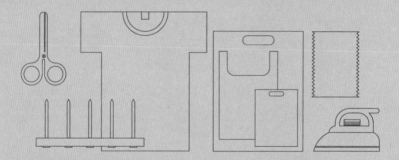

Plastic bag yarn

Yarn made from plastic bags – otherwise known as plarn – is strong, waterproof and durable, and a useful alternative to string in any outdoorsy situation. And while it's not necessarily going to knit into the softest sweater in the world, it works well crocheted into accessories such as belts, braided into trims or just used as is for shoelaces. About ten plastic grocery bags will make a single ball of plarn.

1_ Flatten the bag and cut across horizontally to form a series of loops around 2 cm in width.

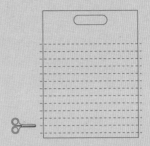

2_ Cut each loop open at one side to make a long strip and then fuse the strips together at the ends using an iron. Cover the plastic with baking parchment before you start ironing.

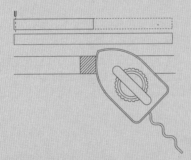

3_ Alternatively, cut the bag into strips horizontally to form a series of loops. Then layer two strips on top of each other and take the loop on the bottom and pull it through itself to form one long string.

4_ Continue adding strips to make a single, very long string. Then wind it into a ball ready to turn all your plarn plans into reality.

T-shirt yarn

Using colourful old T-shirts (ideally logo-free and seam-free where possible), cut the fabric horizontally into loops following the instructions for plarn above. Instead of ironing the ends together, overlap two strips by about 2 cm and stitch a cross shape over them to hold the pieces together.

1_

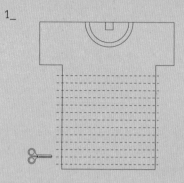

2_

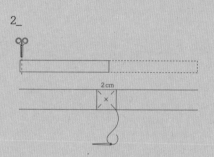

Unravelling a sweater

Salvage the yarn from a one-time favourite sweater and recycle it into a natty new scarf, hat and glove set – or anything else you fancy. Knitted finds from thrift stores can also yield a few balls of beautiful twine even if the original garment is damaged or out of fashion. Usually the newer the sweater, the easier the unravelling will be, as sometimes yarns will begin to cling together with wear. Although the original item doesn't have to be hand-knitted, watch out for cut and seamed garments (check to see if the seams are serged) as these won't unravel completely and will have to be cut, resulting in shorter lengths of yarn. Felted sweaters, mohair and delicate yarns can be more challenging too, so should be reserved for more experienced unravellers.

1_ Turn the sweater inside out.

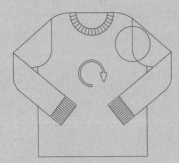

2_ To deconstruct the sweater into its formative parts, find a seam and pull it apart to locate the thread that stitches the parts together. Pull the thread slightly and cut it along the seam, being careful not to cut the yarn in the process.

3_ Taking each component part one by one, start by finding the row of loops at the top from where the knitting was cast off from the needles. A braid of thread may have been put in here originally to stop the knitting unravelling, so remove it by cutting in between the loops (but not the loops themselves).

4_ Look for a small knot at one side of the top row of loops. Cut this knot off (or untie it) and the knitting will begin to unravel.

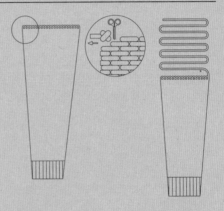

5_ If you come across a serged seam, cut it out using scissors and remove the very short cut lengths of yarn that result before finding the first full line of loops you can.

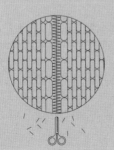

6_ It's not as much fun, but it's sensible to roll the yarn into a ball or onto the niddy-noddy to form a skein as you unravel it. This can save a lot of time untangling later.

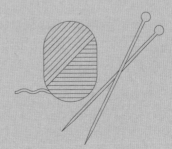

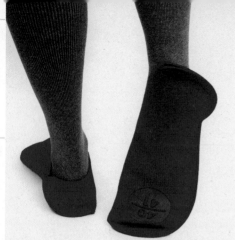

Design example

Emiliana
Felt slippers

Emiliana, the Barcelona-based design studio of Emili Padrós and Ana Mir, is best known for its industrial products and furniture. It was featured in the pages of *Remake It: Home* because of its resourceful upcycling ideas using scooter seats and broom heads. Having established a solid partnership with Spanish manufacturer Nanimarquina designing rugs, the duo saw an opportunity could be underfoot in 2002 when they devised a slipper made from a single piece of wool felt. Cleverly cut and folded, the renewable, biodegradable and utterly loveable Emiliana slippers are held together with just one seam of stitching around the outer edge.

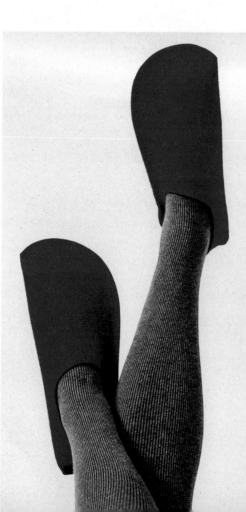

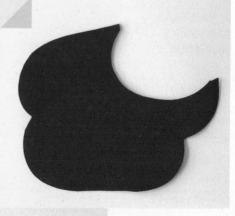

-- Save the vest till last --

The sweater vest (or tank top, as it is known in the UK) has various associations: with the elderly, with the preppy and with unwanted homemade Christmas gifts. Rediscovered by hipsters and held up as a beacon of granny and geek chic, malevolent family members are forced to look elsewhere for embarrassing seasonal gifts these days. The tank top is now a firm contemporary classic. The no-sew way to make one is to felt or shrink a huge old woolly sweater or cardigan by washing it on a hot cycle or (for more control on the shrinkage) boiling it and cutting off the sleeves. A surplus sweater that is not woolly enough to felt properly or large enough to be useful after the inevitable shrinkage, can still be converted into a sweater vest (tank), however, by carefully unpicking the sleeves. Leftover arms can be refashioned into (matching!) socks or leg-warmers.

-- Layer cake --

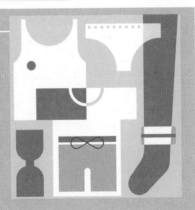

The beauty of lycra and jersey cotton is not only that it cuts down so easily without the need for hemming, but also that it layers brilliantly. As dancers and yoga students model so beautifully, leggings and tights can be cut down into shorts and hot-pants, leotards into two-pieces and T-shirts into tanks and crop tops. All layered over each other, the finished look, multi-coloured, skin-tight and paired with arm-warmers, leg-warmers and headbands, is surely enough to inspire a roomful of remakers to spontaneously break into song and a synchronized sewing routine.

-- Poncho drunk --

The easiest wearable item to make from a large square or circle of textile is a poncho. Particularly practical as a way to reuse bed throws and blankets, this marvellous makeshift Mexican-inspired coverall is also a potential way to upcycle a tablecloth or picnic rug. A shower curtain can also provide good waterproof coverage in the rain. Ponchos are particularly practical for children, who can fall asleep after a long day's running around with a readymade blanket.

MULTIPLE CHOICE

Turn-ups for the book

So many garments can be given a second chance at life through the relatively simple procedure of amputating the legs or arms. It is therefore worth considering the various techniques available to finish up the edges for a truly happy ending.

---

1. The raw edge

_ Many fabrics can survive a raw edge with no intervention – felt and denim being two of them. However, sometimes a raw edge is necessary – or just the desired look – in which case you can give it some longevity in a number of ways.

_ Use an overcast stitch – hand-sew evenly spaced diagonal stitches over and under the fabric edge.

_ Pinking shears will give a fray-resistant scalloped edge.

_ Use a sewing machine to stitch close to the fabric edge – a zigzag stitch will have the same effect as the hand-sewn overcast stitch, while a running stitch will simply neaten the edge.

_ Fray-stop glues are available from most haberdashers and come in liquid or spray form. Starching and ironing the fabric a couple of times can also be effective in the short term (and is sometimes enough for delicate items), and hairspray does much the same job as starch.

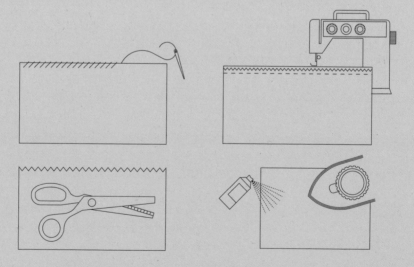

2. The hem

_ Begin by making sure you have measured enough fabric for the hem before cutting the fabric to the new length. A standard hem will use around 2 cm of fabric. If the new hem sits closely to the previous one it will probably be necessary to unpick the first hem.

_ Turn the garment inside out and fold up a centimetre or so to form the hem. One fold is enough if you are working with a thick fabric or don't have much room to manoeuvre, but fold it twice if it won't make it too bulky because the end result will be both tidier and longer lasting. Iron and/or pin the hem in place.

_ Use the machine to sew a straight stitch a few millimetres from the upper-most line of the hem, removing the pins as you go.

3. The mock turn-up

_ This clever procedure is much the same as if you were sewing a normal hem, but it's an effective way to make short-sleeved shirts, trousers and shorts look more polished. Having measured the height you want the turn-ups, turn the garment inside out and fold this amount as if you were making a hem. Fold over again, encasing the raw edge, and iron or pin into place.

_ If you were making a hem, you would now machine a straight stitch along the upper-most line of the hem. But for a turn-up you want to sew along the lower edge.

_ Flip the "hem" out so that it sits on the outside of the garment but press it with an iron to ensure it stays in place.

STEP-BY-STEP

Copy editing

It's one thing to salvage fantastic fabrics from every defunct duvet cover and past-it parachute that make up life's rich tapestry, but the key to real resourcefulness is in also recycling a good design. Making a pattern from an existing garment is the most straightforward way to do this – a process that has the dual benefit of you knowing (loving and fitting) the garment you're remaking, and giving you the chance to alter and improve it in some way. Traditionally, to take the pattern details from a garment it would be necessary to unpick the original at every seam and trace the resulting pieces onto pattern paper. This is still the best method if, for example, the dress in question was found in a thrift store and you want to make it in a different fabric so have no use for the original. However, in many cases the dismantling of a favourite garment is too drastic. And for those situations, there is another way.

You will need:

_ Garment from which to make the new pattern (freshly ironed)
_ A blanket
_ Pins (or a pin-tracing wheel)
_ Ruler
_ French curve
_ Large sheets of paper (baking parchment or tissue paper are better than newspaper for this, as the print may rub off on the fabric)
_ Scissors

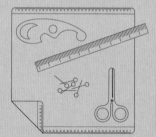

1_ Lay the blanket on the table or floor
and place the paper over the top of it.
Lay the garment to be copied on top
of the paper.

2_ Pin down the garment at the seams
into the blanket.

3_ Carefully mark along the seams for one section by stabbing a pin through the seam and the paper into the blanket (alternatively use a pin-tracing wheel) through the garment.

4_ Unpin the garment and you should have a pattern piece pin-traced onto the paper. Take the paper off the blanket, double check the measurements with a tape measure and redraw the line using a straight ruler or French curve.

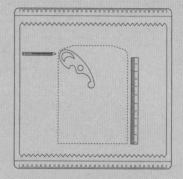

5_ Put the blanket and paper back in place, adjust the garment for another piece and pin again, repeating the process until all the pieces of the garment have been traced.

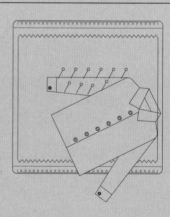

6_ Once you have removed all the pins and finished drawing the lines, draw a second line around 1.5 cm from the edge of each pattern piece you have made. This is the seam allowance.

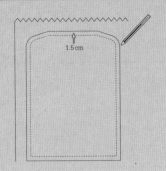

1.5 cm

7_ If the garment has a zip, mark where this fits and remember to make a pattern strip the same length as the zip (plus the seam allowance) in order to reinforce the area where the zip will be sewn in.

8_ Label each pattern piece and mark which way up it should be before cutting them out on this outer line.

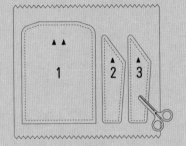

9_ Before you use the pattern double check each piece against the original garment, ensuring all the measurements are correct and you have enough for the seam allowance in each piece.

Walter Raes
Wearable art and design

Belgian-born Walter Raes moved
to London in 1989. It was there
that he became motivated to do
something about the "criminal"
amount of useable waste that he
noticed had become systematic
in cities around the world. Raes
began making wearable art and
designs from these consumer
society throw-outs and his style
eventually evolving to focus, in
particular, on household and
industrial materials that he
frequently recycled from skips.

An intriguing commentary on
the wastefulness of consumer
society, Raes's work makes
much use of the functionality
of his raw materials – the
lacing on discarded trainers
is repurposed in a corset-
like design, while mop heads
substitute for fur on a coat.
And while the original products
are not always immediately
obvious without taking a closer
look, on doing so discoveries
might include electricians' ties,
tampons, baby dummies, ironing
boards or shoe trees – all of
which have made it into his
clothing over the years.

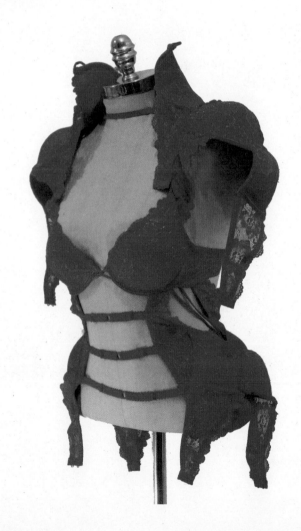

Design example

Walter Raes
Wearable art and design

STEP-BY-STEP

Press for attention

The lowly plastic bag gets bad press these days, thanks to its terrible reputation as a needless environmental scourge. As a result, its financial value has increased: if not yet because of its rarity, but because you are charged for it at the checkout. But given that it may indeed become an endangered species one day, now that so many suppliers, supermarkets and chain stores have started to take measures to reduce its use drastically, the time is ripe to take advantage of this still ubiquitous raw material.

Polyethylene bags have many decorative properties beyond their less welcome adorning of public trees, rivers and walkways. Turning the bags into fabric is one way to exploit that. It is also a useful way to use up a cupboard-full of them, and an oddly enjoyable way to spend a spare hour.

The result of the method outlined here is a Tyvek-like plastic fabric that can be used in a conventional sewing machine and is waterproof, durable and – unless it initially had logos and you make a design feature of them – unrecognizable from its former life as a carrier bag.

Experiment with the technique a few times to perfect it before setting to work on a final design or using up all the best bags in the collection in the beginning. And try different colour combinations and layer different shapes for new effects and patterns. Clear dry-cleaning bags produce a transparent fabric, so you can also trap glitter or small paper pieces between the layers.

You will need:
_ A pile of plastic bags
_ Scissors
_ Iron
_ Baking parchment (you can also substitute newspaper or thin card)
_ Patience

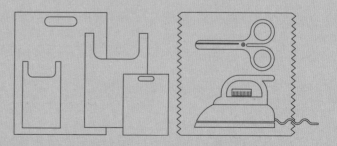

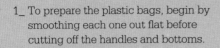

1_ To prepare the plastic bags, begin by smoothing each one out flat before cutting off the handles and bottoms.

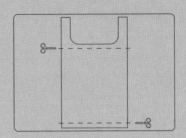

2_ Cut the bags open at one side so that each one is a single flat rectangle of plastic.

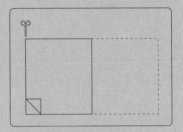

3_ On your ironing board (or another flat surface) arrange the bags in layers of around five to eight sheets on the parchment.

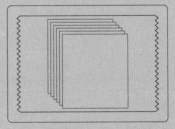

4_ Put another layer of parchment over the top of the bags. Never iron the bags directly as this will just make a sticky plastic mess on the iron and possibly ruin it forevermore.

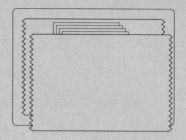

5_ Preheat the iron to a relatively hot setting. The cotton setting works well, but it's worth experimenting first on a small section as irons vary, and the results will depend on the baking parchment you are using or the thickness of the card, as well as the number of layers you are fusing.

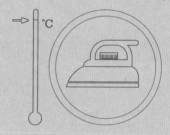

6_ Firmly press the iron on the parchment and run it back and forth enough times to melt the bags and fuse them with each other, but not so much that you cause holes to form in the plastic. This may take a little practice to get right, but if you are using baking parchment you can see what you are doing more easily than with card.

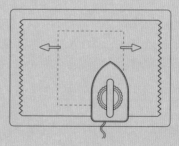

7_ After leaving it to cool for a couple of minutes, remove the parchment slowly and check that there are no areas still left unfused. If there are, just repeat the process.

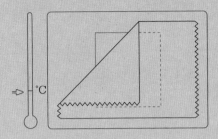

8_ The fabric can then be cut using scissors and sewn on a machine.

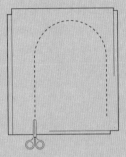

-- Sweat smell of success --

To make sweatbands for the wrists, salvage the ankle section from an otherwise redundant pair of towelling sports socks. Even better – and this will also work for a headband – is to set to work using an old towel and some elastic. Take a length of the elastic and stretch it around your head so that it provides a secure (but not circulation-restricting) fit. Mark and measure this length before releasing the elastic and cutting it with enough material at either end with which to tie it. Next cut a strip of towel the length of the circumference of your head and sew it lengthways into a tube. To make it flat, you can also press it and run the machine along each edge. Turn it the right way around (so the seam is on the inside) and thread the elastic through. Tie the ends of the elastic together up to the marks and sew up the tube.

-- All the trimmings --

Use offcuts of finer fabrics to add subtle detail that will customize and refresh an otherwise tired item of clothing. Line a pocket, a collar or a cuff in a beautiful, colourful lightweight textile that only the wearer will know is there. Or add discreet but chic ties on a sleeve to hold a turn-up more neatly. Match them to a new set of button loops or perhaps a pocket flap on an otherwise plain garment. Cut into thin, ribbon-like strips – silk or gauze can be sewn as a barely-there trim around the neckline and cuffs of a dress, jacket or blouse and immediately give it a new look and a more luxurious feel – a trick that also even works with an old T-shirt after cutting off the hems and neckline.

-- Time to reflect --

Reflective fabrics and straps – often found on specialist sportswear – can be salvaged along with offcuts from neon protective wear and reused as both practical and decorative strips for many occasions. You can try sewing it into detachable hoods, remaking larger pieces into ponchos and collars to provide extra visibility while cycling, or fashioning straps into belts, bracelets and armbands that can also be worn off-road. Stripes of the fabric can also be added onto running gear or incorporated onto trainers for safer night-time jogs.

-- Fobbed off --

Of course anything, within reason, can be adapted to make a keyfob, but as a checklist it should be hardwearing, tactile and easy to spot (but not too large or heavy). Suggestions could be a cut of leather from an old belt or perhaps a string of beads or stones taken from a broken piece of jewelry. Small toys, light pulls and tools such as torches and bottle openers are all tried and tested classics, as is the carabiner, the climbers' clip, but there's plenty of scope to be inventive still. Drill a hole through the top of a Kinder Surprise plastic egg and thread a loop of strong string through it for an instant portable pillbox or adapt an empty mirrored makeup compact, using the empty tray to hold messages, mantras, emergency numbers or photographs.

-- Flexible footwear --

Reincarnation is not just for yogis, but also their mats. And for the next life, what every yoga mat aspires to is rebirth as a pair of flip-flops. After scrubbing down the mat, trace a sole shape from an existing pair of flip-flops or trainers onto the surface. Cut five soles for each foot and, using a hot-glue gun, bond four of them together (make sure the textured side is face down). Standing on the last of the five soles, make a mark on the rubber between the big and second toes before cutting a slit where the mark is using a Stanley knife. For the uppers, another strip of yoga mat will work well, but a braided strip of fabric offcuts is possibly a more comfortable alternative. Thread this through the hole, looping around the sole and up over again, pushing the other end into the same slit. Try it on and adjust for comfort before gluing down the ends on the reverse. Finally, add the last layer of sole to the stack, pressing down extra firmly to eliminate lumps and bumps as much as possible.

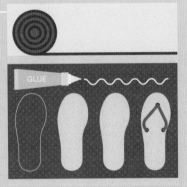

STEP-BY-STEP

All that glitters

Like making the pasta for a lasagne from scratch, the idea of homemade sequins could seem a little extreme for anyone but the most dedicated dressmaker. It's not strictly speaking necessary, and it could easily take all day. But, like the lasagne, not only is the end result more impressive and satisfying, but also the possibilities for variation are endless.

You will need:

_ Thin plastic packaging or stationery files, old compact disks, laminated paper, redundant Christmas decorations, photographic film or colour filters or tape (stick two layers of tape together or stick it over a plastic bag or pages from an old magazine and so on)

_ A hole punch (traditional or novelty) or a pair of scissors
_ A thick, but sharp, needle such as that used for upholstery
_ Needle and thread for sewing

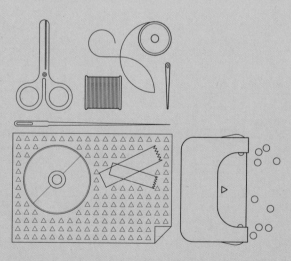

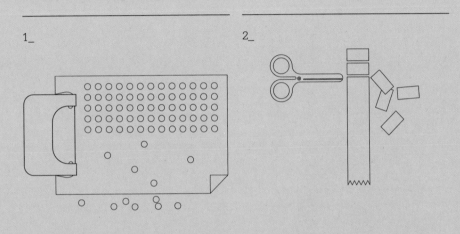

1_ Select the material to be used and punch as many holes in it as possible, collecting the circles at the end.
2_ Alternatively, cut the material into oblongs or squares using scissors.
3_ Pierce holes in the centre of the punched circles using the upholstery needle. If working with oblongs, the best position for the hole is at the top edge.
4_ Sew the sequins onto the garment in horizontal layers, starting at the bottom edge of the area to be covered. Then work your way up.

1_

2_

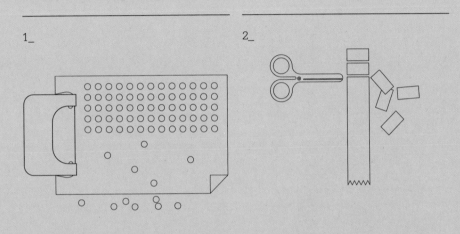

3_

4_

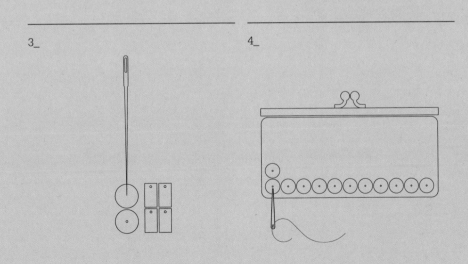

Suzanne Lee
BioCouture

While there are many pioneers of the reduce, reuse, recycle approach to sustainable fashion and textiles, London-based academic Suzanne Lee began exploring an altogether different route: grow your own.

While working at London's Central Saint Martins College of Art and Design, Lee initiated the BioCouture programme, which uses microbes to grow biomaterials, so negating the traditional need to create fabric from either plants or petrochemicals. Lee's researchers add a mixed culture of bacterial cellulose, yeasts and other micro-organisms to a sugary green tea solution. The bacteria feed on the sugar and spin fine threads of cellulose which, as they start to stick together, form a skin on the liquid's surface. After two to three weeks a flexible cellulose mat approximately 1.5 cm thick, with leather-like qualities, is produced. This can be moulded onto a 3D form or dried flat and used as a material.

Lee discovered that the BioCouture fabric could be dyed and printed, and since it requires far less dye than other fibres has considerable environmental advantages. Best of all, like vegetable peelings, it can be safely composted at the end of its life.

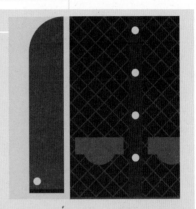

-- Shrink to fit --

Tailoring an old pair of jeans into a new cut and style is an easy way to refresh a look. Slim a wide-legged pair down into skinnies or a straight-leg design, for example, by taking in each side a little. As with all alterations, the way to success here is to tack the new seams in place by hand first and try the jeans on repeatedly until you're happy with them before sewing securely on a machine. For the type of skinny that looks as though it's been sewn on, leave an opening of about 20 cm on the outside seam at the ankle so that a zip can be added later to make sure they can still be pulled on over the foot.

-- Gilet stakes --

Removing the sleeves from an outdated denim or leather jacket can create an infinitely more serviceable gilet (or vest), but it's a trick that can also work well for a padded or quilted jacket, a suit jacket or a blazer. In the case of a suit jacket, it's not a bad idea to consult a tailor first, but with a little creative adaptation – shortening the bottom edge, removing the lapels, resizing for a tailored fit and finish and possibly adding a new back panel in silk – the fabric and structure will move (if not entirely seamlessly) into a new life as a waistcoat.

-- How cold my toes --

Many people prefer to eschew slippers for a pair of thick socks while padding around the house, but although they may be comfortable they are also slippery, quickly wear thin and can get damp or dirty fast. Cue the amazing invention that is the slippersock: a sock with the simple addition of a soft sole, giving it traction, warmth and durability without compromising the otherwise perfect sock look and feel. With the socks on, trace around the feet onto a piece of card, cut out the templates and use them to transfer the shape onto a spare piece of suede or other more hardwearing fabric such as an old rug or thin matting. Take off the socks and stitch the sole to their bases.

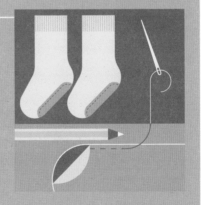

STEP-BY-STEP

Pigment of the imagination

Using household bleach is a fast and easy way to give a coloured garment a new, edgier look, while cunningly removing stains at the same time. When it comes to creating a whitewash of a situation, that bottle under the sink can put any communist dictator to shame in micro seconds: bleach is a useful tool but one to be used with care, rubber gloves, overalls and held breath. Decide on a design before starting – splatters and splashes à la Jackson Pollock or a "starry night" look on a black dress. You can also spritz bleach over a cutout template shape.

You will need:

_ Garment to be bleached
_ Freezer paper
_ Scissors
_ Cardboard
_ Bleach solution (dilute one part bleach to one part water)
_ Spray bottle
_ Iron

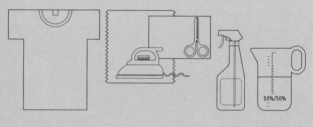

1_ Draw a graphic design onto freezer paper and cut it out to make a template. Bear in mind the fabric's potential to "bleed" when choosing a design as it can be tricky to get very defined detail in some cases.
2_ Iron the template onto the garment, waxy side down.
3_ Use a piece of card under the top layer of the garment to prevent bleach leaking through to the other side.
4_ Transfer the bleach solution into a plant sprayer or old pump-action toiletries spray bottle and spray it over and around the template. Use as little as possible to get the wanted effect as bleach and dyes can sometimes deteriorate fabric fibres as well as dissolve their colour.
5_ Watch as the pigment disappears around the template and leave to dry for a couple of minutes before peeling off the freezer paper.
6_ Wash the garment thoroughly as soon as possible to remove all traces of bleach before wearing it.

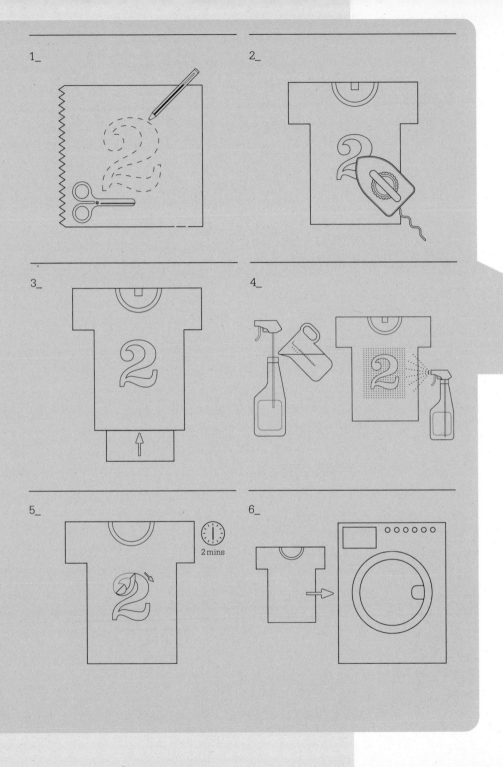

1_

2_

3_

4_

5_

2 mins

6_

-- Trim up --

The most traditional way to revamp an old garment is by customizing it along the edges with the addition of fringes, ribbons, buttons or brocade. Or all of the above, for those who like life on the edge. A failsafe practice, the best part of experimenting with new designs in this way is that if it doesn't work, you can always unpick it all and start again. Swap buttons from other garments or make new ones – it's also a good idea to use fabric scraps to make covered buttons that match or contrast. Trims and fringes can be homemade using scraps, so it's worth keeping a dedicated basket to safekeep likely looking salvaged ribbons and bindings – often posh boutique carrier bags feature luxurious handles that can be saved, for example, and, on occasion, giftwrapping can keep on giving much longer than the present itself.

-- Revision time --

Beading, embroidery, patches and studs are brilliant options when resuscitating old items – and can be particularly useful as a means of covering up stains, tears or moth holes in prominent places. You can find inspiration and ideas by investigating different cultures and traditions from around the world. Sketch out designs on paper – and then on the garment itself – before starting work. The key to success here is in thinking it through, as well as making sure any adornment being added won't overwhelm the garment or affect the way it hangs by being too heavy for the original fabric.

-- Dye hard (with a vengeance) --

Shellfish, insects, lichen, roots, barks, leaves, berries, fungi and vegetables have all been used throughout history to bring colour to cloth. As concerns about the health and environmental impacts of synthetic dyes increase there is a growing resurgence for a practice that, in China, has been traced back more than 5,000 years. Remarkably, the process of dyeing has changed little over time – and essentially entails boiling the material to be used as the dye in a pot of water before the textiles to be coloured are added and stirred on the heat. In order to fix the pigment, many natural dye mordants can be used to bind the dye to the textile fibres; they can be created using, for instance, salt, vinegar, cream of tartar or ammonia (from stale urine). Instructions and colour guides are readily available in published form online and off, but for the best results experimentation is highly recommended (see the step-by-step on pages 130–131).

Yellow – fresh birch leaves
Gold – birch bark
Olive yellow – heather flower shoots
Grey – blackberries
Green – bracken shoots, elder leaves
Lilac – elderberries
Brown – walnut husks and shells, oak bark
Reddish yellow – pine cones
Pink – dried madder, beetroot

-- Retweet --

A feather trim is a detail that can instantly add glamour and ethereal grace to an otherwise tired or dull garment – whether it's an old evening dress or a simple T-shirt. Fiddly to sew on individually, an easier method is to align the feathers on a sheet of tissue paper before machine sewing them across the base. The tissue paper can then be carefully torn away, leaving the feathers joined as a thread which can then be pinned and sewn onto or into the garment. For a fuller look, rows of feather strings can be layered up together. Experiment with different feather types and colours, depending on what's available without bothering the budgie.

-- Sparkling conversation --

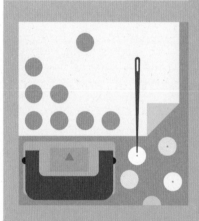

Sequins are generally considered to be partywear – but just as every true rebel knows sunglasses don't strictly need to be reserved for sunny weather, a little razzle dazzle shouldn't need to be limited to after dark. Coordinating with the disco ball is not the only purpose of covering clothes with these tiny light-spinning discs – sequins can just as happily add a little pizzazz to everyday wear and are a fast and easy way to upgrade a T-shirt, in particular. Shop-bought sequins are available in every colour and many shapes and sizes, but making a batch at home opens up more possibilities still: use a hole punch on plastic sheeting, laminated paper or empty packaging for traditional-scale sequins, or take some scissors to old CDs to make bigger, abstract shapes and to create futurama fashions of Paco Rabanne circa 1960 (see also the step-by-step on pages 156–57).

One of the most efficient ways to make use of scrap fabric is to build it together into a greater whole through patchwork. It can then be used as a regular length of fabric to make clothes, bags and other accessories. Many designers of reclaimed clothing use this technique, often making their creative mark through distinctive patching forms as well as through the cut and style of their final garments, which rely on the lay of the patchwork for their shape as well as their intrigue. Patchwork is usually based on repeat patterns using different-coloured geometric shapes that are easy to tile together, but there are many variations and traditional styles. "Strip piecing" involves stitching pieces of fabric together into long strips and then stitching these lengths together. Careful measuring and cutting is crucial in building a good patchwork, so that the result lies flat and the joins don't pucker. The earliest examples of patchwork have been discovered in Egyptian tombs and the technique has proved invaluable ever since – having been used in the construction of armour in the Middle Ages to keep soldiers that little bit cosier on the battlefield and, more recently, as a basis for much remaking during the textile shortages of the Second World War.

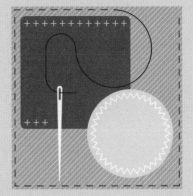

ACCESSORIES

Belts, buckles, hats, gloves, leg-warmers,
slippers, bags, flip-flops, bow ties and earmuffs

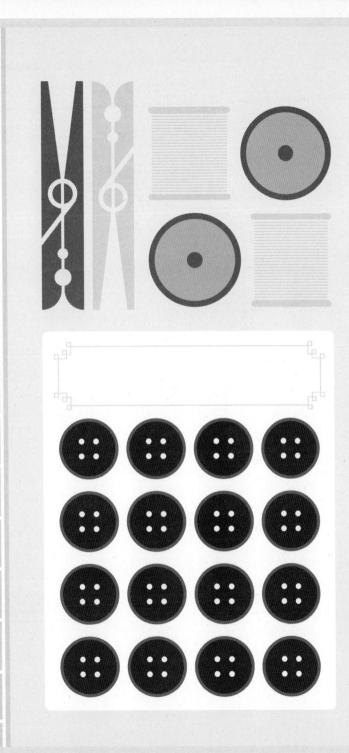

-- Bootie call --

The never-ending usefulness of the odd sock continues with its easy reappropriation into a mobile phone cosy: an effective anti-theft security measure and scratch protector in one. A small child's sock or baby bootie might do the job with little to no adaptation at all, but with a little deft tailoring even a giant-sized rugby sock can be ceremoniously converted. Measure the phone against the fabric – you want the elastic to be a couple of centimetres from the top of the phone – and cut off any surplus sock at the bottom. Turn it inside out and run the sewing machine across the cut end; narrow the side seam to give a snug fit. Wash before use.

-- Human beanies --

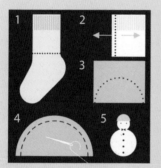

Feel the creative remaking energy flowing directly from the tips of your toes to the top of your head and refashion a pair of holey socks into a beanie hat. Start by cutting off the feet, then open out the side of the remaining tube to form a flat, woolly square. Leaving the elastic edge as the straight edge, cut a semi-circle roughly the size of half your head from each sock. Place the two pieces back to back so any stripes are aligned and sew a running stitch around the curved edge to form a tea-cosy shape. Turn it back the right way again and settle in.

-- Cut some rug --

Since the 19th century, carpets – especially oriental rugs – have been recycled into travelling bags of all shapes and sizes that are renowned for their durability and resistance to stains and other wear and tear. Various patterns are available for making them at home, and although these usually require a frame this can always be appropriated from another old bag or bought from a good haberdashery store. The other option is the simpler, folded form of a "railway rug". Used during Victorian times to lend warmth in drafty, unheated railcars in Europe and the US, the rug could be opened out as a blanket or latched up on the sides using leather straps to make a travelling bag. A basic lining will stop the contents from falling out and may provide another good use for a pillowcase.

Bernstock Speirs
Bubblewrap accessories

Giving new meaning to the term "protective clothing", Bernstock Speirs is a millinery label that understands the eccentricities of the British hat-wearing public well. With a nod to the ladies' rainhats of the 1970s, and a wink at the traditions of make do and mend, the bubblewrap hat was launched in 2010 to help maintain a little dry humour come wet weather.

The London-based label was established in 1982 by Paul Bernstock and Thelma Speirs, who met while studying Fashion/ Textiles at Middlesex University. Their mission was to herald in a new generation of hat wearers, and they quickly succeeded with their well-made styles and witty twists on traditional shapes and use of unconventional fabrics and techniques.

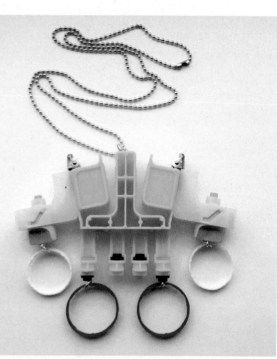

Design example
Plastic Seconds
Trashy treasure

Whether in bottle tops, Biro lids or soy sauce fishes, Maria Papadimitriou finds beauty in some unlikely places. But for the designer behind Plastic Seconds, it's all a matter of context. After graduating with a fine art degree, Papadimitriou was compelled to make jewelry from commonly disregarded plastic parts when she discovered that so many everyday items – for example, plastic bottle tops – are difficult to recycle in conventional ways and so would otherwise be likely to go straight to landfill. For her popular eco-accessory line she now collects packaging parts to reuse as beads, and fashions colourful rings from the bases of shampoo and detergent bottles.

Design example
Fallon Jewelry
Speakerwire resort collection
Once Fallon Jewelry's designer
Dana Lorenz saw the success
of the crystal, pearl and
speakerwire necklace she
created for the CFDA Swarovski
Award Collection in 2010, she
was inspired to take the idea
further and launch the first-
ever resort collection for the
brand. Exploring the clash of
traditional jewelry ideas with the
less conventional material that
is speakerwire, Lorenz devised
a 25-piece range that featured
"Wire Management", beribboned
earrings resembling tied cables,
"Speed of Light", a spike and
crystal necklace, and "Sound
Bite" stud earrings, all of which
struck the right note with her
customers, whose good feedback
resonated at an appropriately
serious volume.

Margot Bowman
Fashion illustration

An illustrator, designer and DJ living in London, Margot Bowman was already gaining multiple prestigious commissions from magazines and brands (such as Topshop and Urban Outfitters) while in her final year of a graphic design course at Central Saint Martins College of Art and Design in London. Her multi-disciplinary approach covers illustration, digital and screenprinting, large-scale paintings, product and clothing designs, as well as a popular series of quirky animated fashion GIFs. This is one of the most significant keys to her success: working across so many different visual languages allows her to use her medium to best convey the right message.

"It's not about being the first anymore, it's about how well and how effectively you can interact with that media or that information," she said in one interview. Where her medium is clothing, Bowman takes otherwise dull or plain garments and uses them as a basic canvas, painting and drawing directly onto the fabric.

-- Insole searching --

To add support and comfort to any footwear, a homemade insole can help provide a better fit and eliminate any unsavoury cheese odours just as well as any shop-bought version. Felt, with its wonderful warmth and wicking ability, is always a good plan underfoot, while other options include rubber inner-tubing (easily washable), craft foam or offcuts from that old pair of Wellington boots – from that time they were cut down to make that pair of Croc-alikes for the garden...so it was a good idea after all...

-- Digital access --

Fingerless gloves make a style statement with both the Dickensian pickpocket look and the 1980s rebel-girl popstar. Making fingerless gloves from an old perhaps one-time full-fingered pair is clearly just a case of chopping off the last remaining digits. To stop edges on woolly gloves fraying, it is advisable to sew a running stitch just below where you want to cut beforehand. To secure them further afterwards, roll over the ends slightly and secure with a blanket stitch or whip stitch by hand. For a more "Madonna circa 1985 in *Desperately Seeking Susan*" look, take a pair of lace tights and cut them off at the heel. Cut off a leg section as long you want the resulting gloves to be and make a hole near the narrowest end (the ankle) for your thumb.

-- Crime cycle --

To achieve a bank-robber look on a budget, an instant balaclava can be improvised by using an old pair of semi-opaque tan or black tights. For the smarter, more professional organized criminal, however, a more pre-considered version can be made using the sleeve of an old sweater or fleece. Cut and finish the holes – either just for the eyes or a larger opening for the whole face. This will give less anonymity, of course, so better for cold-weather sporting and leisure pursuits than criminal ones.

-- Leather forecast --

There's an unspoken law of the universe which dictates that a single glove lost from a pair is always the same hand as the glove that got lost from the last pair too, thus damning the ones left behind to oddness forever in eternity. But every cloud has a silver lining, etc. Actually, it's not the lining in this case that provides the benefit: it can be totally removed from a lone leather glove prior to its upcycling into leather cuffs and rings. Snip the fingers off at the base and cut the tips off to form tubes slightly bigger than the size required before repairing and securing any loose stitching by hand so that it won't unravel. Boil the resulting tubes for a few minutes in a pan of water. Remove them from the water, shape the forms and leave to dry – the leather will harden during this process. Once the rings are dried and hardened, they can be embellished with metallic leather paint, beads or stones for an instant digital upgrade.

-- Wrap stars --

Upcycle a length of fabric that is too beautiful to cut up by turning it into a stole for evening wear. This is a good way to show off a strong pattern or fine textile, so old bedspreads and throws lend themselves particularly well to the cause, as do kimonos, kaftans and other textile remnants or scraps. Measure, mark and cut the material into a long rectangle – about 90 by 180 cm – and do the same with a lining fabric, ideally slipper satin. Pin the right sides together and use a running stitch to sew three sides of the rectangle together. Turn it out the right way again, press it, turn the edges of the last seam in and lightly hand-stitch it closed before adding an optional fringe, tassels or embroidery.

-- A good shrink --

A bucket bag, combined with handles and buckle from scrap leather trimmings – perhaps an old leather belt – is another practical and rewarding use for industrial felt. A shrunken felted woollen sweater can also be used with the T-shirt tote design (see pages 180–81) to make a strong shopper in a similar vein. For extra protection and a longer-lasting result add a leather base to the design, as well as feet, which can be made using salvaged hardware such as large screws, nuts and bolts (punch holes in the leather and thread through) or metal studs.

Design example
Marloes ten Bhömer
Bluemâchéshoe

Design for the extremities doesn't get more extreme than Marloes ten Bhömer. Trained at the Higher School of Arts, Arnhem and the Royal College of Art in London, the Dutch designer's conceptual footwear has more in common with contemporary architecture than conventional womenswear and fashion, fusing cutting edge technologies and innovative manufacturing processes with lines an origami expert would envy. Foot binding made fabulous for the 21st century, her leather-mâché technique is leather lamination. The form of the Bluemâchéshoe follows the form of the foot on the inside, but has a radical, sculptural silhouette externally.

Design example
Marloes ten Bhömer
Bluemâchéshoe

STEP-BY-STEP

Green T bags

This is about as easy as making a cup of tea, but it has the advantage
of staying hot for quite a bit longer and you can dunk whole packets
of biscuits in it at once. These three simple steps will transform an
old T-shirt into a new tote bag in a matter of minutes.

You will need:

_ An old T-shirt
_ Thread
_ Sewing machine
_ Card to make a template
  or a dinner plate
_ Scissors
_ Pins
_ Chalk pencil

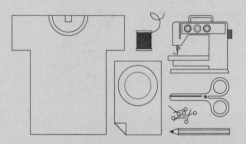

1_ Iron the T-shirt flat before cutting off the
sleeves. Leave the seam intact for extra
strength because the new armholes are
going to be the bag handles.

2_ Cut a deep round opening for the bag
at the neck of the T-shirt, making sure
it is even on both the front and back.
You could use a dinner plate or make
your own template from card.

3_ Turn the T-shirt inside out and pin
and sew across the base – go over
the stitches a couple of times to
reinforce them. Turn it back the right
way again and suddenly, magically,
you have a bag.

4_ For extra storage space, refashion the
old sleeves into patch pockets.

While this remake is perfect for lighter
loads, for a sturdier, reversible shoulder
bag double up the T-shirts first.

_ Turn one of the T-shirts inside out and
arrange it so that it sits inside the other,
insides facing.

_ Mark and cut the sleeves and neckhole
together so that they match up.
The easiest way to do this is to use
a template such as a dinner plate to
draw around on each side.

_ Sew these securely together using
a zigzag stitch. First go around each
armhole and then the bag opening
at the neck.

_ To make the bag fully reversible, stitch
up the bases independently from each
other – turning each one inside out
first. This way you won't be left with
an unfinished seam whichever way
you want to wear it.

1_

2_

3_

4_

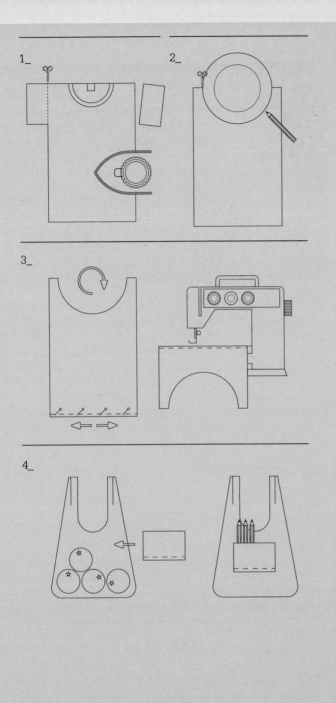

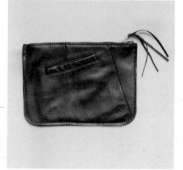

Design example
Shannon South
reMade USA

New York-based Shannon South has turned emotional baggage into a business opportunity. Moved to set up her handmade handbag business in 2009, South had become increasingly disillusioned with mass-production methods when she stumbled across a rugged old leather jacket in a Goodwill store and had the idea of transforming it into a bag. Many more Goodwill jackets followed, as did a stream of eager customers and deals with some of the US's most prestigious fashion and department stores.

South works the bags herself, by hand, letting the details of the garment guide the design and using as much of the jacket leather as possible in the process. Every tote, clutch and satchel is different from the next and customers also submit their own jackets – often sentimentally valuable, but for one reason or another unwearable in their current state.

A strict vegetarian, the designer chooses to work with discarded leather for its resilience and durability, as well as the deeper layer of value in the material – the new bags carry the weight of history.

STEP-BY-STEP

Take a bow

Politicians, architects, pediatricians and clowns – just some of the professionals who have become associated with bow-tie wearing. And how an accessory can bring to mind the eccentric, the iconoclast and the car salesman all at once is as much a mystery as trying to tie one. This version is not only far less fiddly, but also closer to the original item (when bow ties were originally invented and used a simple straight strip of cloth) so possibly it could claim to be a little bit classier than faking it with a spinning bow on elastic. Though those are good, too, admittedly... All that needs to be conjured up is an ordinary tie and extraordinary cunning, with minimal expertise required.

You will need:

_ A tie (this can be any fabric, but the width will determine the size of the end result)

1_ Lay the tie on a flat surface face down. Take the wide end, fold it up and tuck the point into the label.
2_ Thinking of the label as the centre of the bow tie, take the other end of the tie and fold it back on itself.
3_ Repeat this going back in the other direction, so you have a concertina effect of three layers.
4_ Folding it back on itself one final time, take the length of the tie at the centre of the pile and fold it on the diagonal,

before wrapping it once around the pile to form a bow shape.
5_ Tuck the length through itself at the back of the bow.
6_ Use the long length to tie the bow tie around the neck, finally securing the end by tucking it under itself at the side.

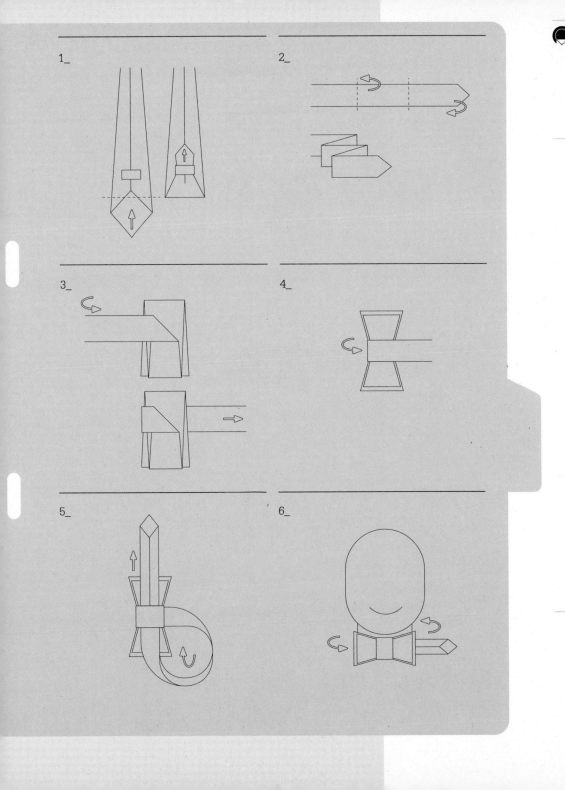

1_

2_

3_

4_

5_

6_

Something's Hiding in Here
Forage bow ties

A hand-carved wooden moustache-on-a-stick and original letterpressed stationery: Something's Hiding in Here is a Philadelphia-based design duo with several impressive products under their decidedly steampunk belts. But the biggest break for the couple came with the launch in 2010 of Forage – a collection of handmade limited edition bow ties.

The ties are fashioned from vintage fabrics into designs inspired by eminent bow-tie wearers from history such as Charles Eames, Le Corbusier and Louis Kahn, and the decision to launch the range was partly in the spirit of encouraging this "most practical form of neckwear" – a must-have for the creative, a bow tie won't interfere with machinery (or lunch) like a dangling neck tie might. Not stopping at recycling fabrics, Forage's tags are also made from vintage monogram tags from Italy, while the designers hand-print the packaging themselves on a vintage letterpress and build display stands using reclaimed architectural spindles and timber.

-- Fancy footwork --

So many panels, so many possibilities – pimping a pair of sneakers is a great way to bring some fresh colour to old treads and is invariably a fun and satisfying process, guaranteeing you get your creative kicks (in every sense of the word). For canvas sneakers paint markers are best for the job or for leather there are several good brands of leather paints available. Water-based acrylics are also commonly used, but treat the sneaker first using acetone. Remove the laces and mark out the design with a pencil, and as an extra precaution (essential if spray painting) also mark off the areas not to be painted using masking tape. Afterwards seal with a product such as Mod Podge to make it last longer.

-- Collar me beautiful --

Detach and keep a collar from an old shirt and reuse it as an alternative neckpiece – a look that can work as well (perhaps better) over plain T-shirts and simple dresses as it can in its original context on a troop of buff naked torsos on a stage in Soho. Old dress shirts and accompanying bow ties are only one option – lighter collars of all shapes can be salvaged from blouses or made from scratch using up scrap fabric or vintage fur. Where there is no button or fastening, add a ribbon tie.

-- It's a cinch --

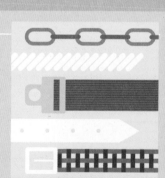

How long is a piece of string? Quite often, long enough to make a belt with. But the ways to cinch a waist, hoist a trouser or pull together a toga are as infinite as there are types of scrap and belt buckles. All manner of odd lengths of fabric or leather, from an old bag strap to binding tape, can be refashioned into a belt, on their own, knotted or braided into a new strip, giving built-in "holes" for use with a buckle with a centre pin. Elastic webbing, salvaged from upholstered furniture, can be refashioned with the addition of a clasp or poppers, as can hardware chains or specialist ropes, curtain ties or even a seatbelt can be ingeniously upcycled with the addition of a natty clasp or buckle.

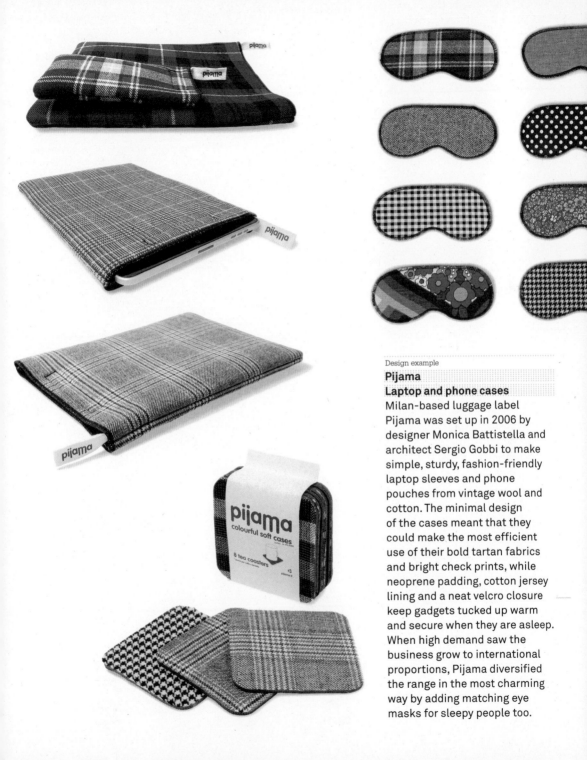

Design example

Pijama
Laptop and phone cases

Milan-based luggage label
Pijama was set up in 2006 by
designer Monica Battistella and
architect Sergio Gobbi to make
simple, sturdy, fashion-friendly
laptop sleeves and phone
pouches from vintage wool and
cotton. The minimal design
of the cases meant that they
could make the most efficient
use of their bold tartan fabrics
and bright check prints, while
neoprene padding, cotton jersey
lining and a neat velcro closure
keep gadgets tucked up warm
and secure when they are asleep.
When high demand saw the
business grow to international
proportions, Pijama diversified
the range in the most charming
way by adding matching eye
masks for sleepy people too.

Design example

Sägen Butik
Crockery collection

Inspired by the memory of shared family dinners at her grandmother's house, Swedish jewelry designer Elin Sigrén uses discarded crockery as the basis for her simple nostalgic pieces. Necklaces, brooches, earrings and hair accessories are fashioned from porcelain tableware that Sigrén finds at local fleamarkets before grinding the forms by hand into large geometric shapes and setting them in silver.

Initially established in 2007, Sägen Butik's collections grew to incorporate accessories made from vintage buttons and textiles. Sigrén puts the popularity of the porcelain pieces down to their link to a bygone era at a time when sitting down to a traditional family meal is ever rarer.

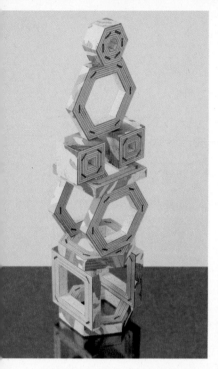

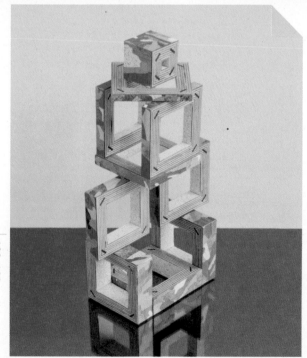

Design example

Bethan Laura Wood
Particle collection

Since graduating from the Royal College of Art in London, Bethan Laura Wood has established her own practice, WOOD London, designing and producing bespoke products ranging from furniture and ceramics to jewelry, as well as collaborating on large-scale projects and completing a number of residencies at galleries and exhibitions worldwide. Her Particle rings and jewelry pieces evolved from a large-scale furniture project of the same name with wood laminate and formica offcuts worked into complex and intricate lacquered mosaic surfaces.

The Particle Collection includes bracelets, bangles and rings, all fashioned in geometric shapes with limited edition runs.

Design example
Henrik Vibskov
Car-seat accessories
Henrik Vibskov epitomizes the
"slash/slash" generation: artist/
fashion designer/drummer/
perfumer/set creator – but
whatever he puts his mind to the
result somehow seems to imply
that he's had a lot of fun doing it.
King of Copenhagen's subversive
fashion scene, unusual and
upcycled materials feature
frequently in Vibskov's designs,
but never in a way that you are
likely to see anywhere else. The
car-seat laptop sleeve is a case
in point.

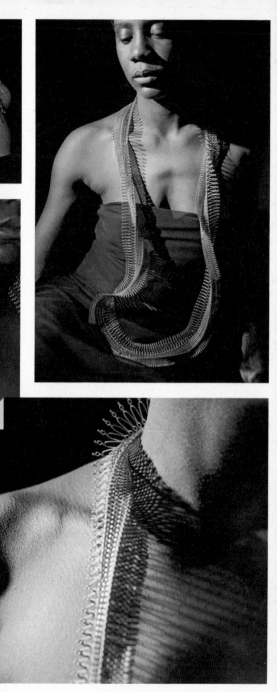

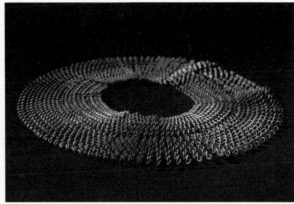

Florie Salnot
Plastic bottle project

The Saharawis were once a nomadic people who lived in Western Sahara until 1975 when their territory was annexed by Morocco. Since then, more than half of the Saharawis have been living in exile in a barren and remote stretch of Algerian desert while the rest live under Moroccan occupation. While the Saharawis used to have a craft tradition, this was quickly lost due to a lack of resources (such as leather) and dwindling sales opportunities.

The Plastic Bottle Project was developed by French designer Florie Salnot while she was studying at the Royal College of Art in London. She had studied History of Art and Anthropology and Cabinet-Making in Paris. Passionate about applying design in ways that can address social issues, in this instance Salnot was looking for opportunities to give the refugee Saharawi people more independence from humanitarian help and a means of self expression. Her solution was to devise a new technique and tools to produce jewelry using the very limited resources available in the camps – essentially just plastic bottles and sand.

The plastic bottle is painted before being cut into thin strips, which can then be wound around a nail board to create patterns and drawings. The whole is then submerged into hot sand, causing the plastic strip to shrink, keeping the shape of the pattern into which it has been formed. With a few last steps and fittings, the simple technique sees the plastic waste transformed into fine and precious jewelry.

MULTIPLE CHOICE

Go go gadget
- - - - - - - - - - - - - - - - -

The show-off factor is entirely related to the difficulty rating when it comes to homemade laptop and phone cases, so making them very attractive to anyone who feels the urge to get hands on and create something useful. At least a thousand Etsy shopkeepers can testify to this. The only problem standing in the way of glory and a bespoke, hand-crafted personal gadget covering is deciding on a design. Here are some starting points:

1. The Jiffy Bag

The ultimate in laptop security, the humble Jiffy padded envelopes come in a range of standard sizes, many of which just happen to fit a 13-inch laptop, a tablet or phone perfectly. Choose a discretely used envelope just with your address on it in case of loss or decorate it with printed graphics. There are also coloured and metallic versions for disco days.

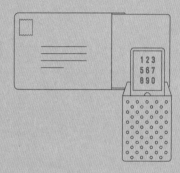

2. Blanket

The thickness and durability of woollen blankets make them well suited to protecting and insulating electronic accessories. Associated with both wintery nights and summery picnics, the results are also trans-seasonal, appropriate whether you need to whip it out for fireside web browsing, BBMing on the beach or are in need of some in-car navigation on a country lane.

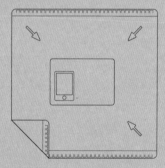

3. Sweater

An outgrown child's chunky knitted sweater can be refashioned to keep a laptop as snug as a bug in a rug (which might also, incidentally, do the job another time) with minimum intervention. Cut off the arms and sew up the armholes, adjusting the width as necessary. The sleeves can be made into a matching phone case or two.

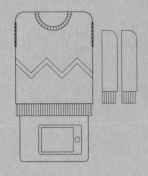

4. Hot water bottle cover

As above, the humble hot water bottle cover should be around the right size for a laptop or tablet – the only minor adaptation needed is to fold down or cut off the allowance made for the spout.

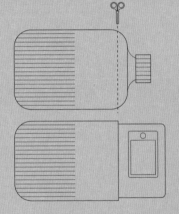

5. Leather

Leather (perhaps salvaged from a thrift-store jacket) makes a traditional, sophisticated and durable case for electronics that will wear well over time and protect the device/s from scratches and marks without adding bulk to your luggage.

6. Wetsuit neoprene

Like leather, neoprene cut from a worn-out or outgrown wetsuit provides a second skin for a laptop or phone (see the step-by-step on pages 200– 203), although with a slightly sportier look. Ideal for web surfers.

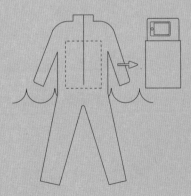

Design example
959
Seatbelt accessories
In 1959, Volvo became the first car manufacturer to install the three-point seatbelt in its cars as a standard item, so changing forever the idea of car safety. Fifty years later, the move would also provide inspiration to one Paolo Ferrari, an industrial designer, who launched 959, a collection of upcycled seatbelt accessories. Ferrari, a graduate of the Politecnico di Milano, had long been exploring the recuperation and reuse of industrial objects and transforming them into fashion or design articles. 959 is constructed entirely with material from car scrap yards – giving an unexpected new lease of life to the polyester belts that have been deliberately designed to be as indestructible and strong as possible.

TRAIDremade
Golightly shoes

TRAIDremade is a sustainable
label set up by the fashion
recycling charity TRAID to make
good use of unwanted and
damaged textiles. All of the items
– shoes, clothes and accessories
– are handmade in Brighton.
The design and pattern-making

are kept fluid to fit with the
constraints and unpredictability
of working with reused materials.

The only exception are
TRAIDremade's "Golightly" ballet
flats. A range of shoes launched
in 2011, they are made entirely
from scrap leather and fabric
remnants and are manufactured
in factories in East London and
Norwich. The key challenge

for the makers was to create
matching pairs using only small
batches of often highly patterned
vintage textiles.

TRAID donates all of its profits
to projects challenging poverty in
the global textile industry.

STEP-BY-STEP

Laptop cover

Considering that it may be one of the simplest accessories to make, it is surprising how long it took for manufacturers and fashion houses to start producing good looking and high-quality laptop sleeves and phone cases. Actually, it took them precisely as long as it took Apple to launch the iPad. But no matter. While they were busy pondering whether personal technology was really worth wrapping up in pretty packages, the tech geeks (ever the pioneers when it comes to remaking and generally "life hacking") were making their own. It follows, then, that to wrap up some tech in a homemade package is to celebrate the original geek chic. Here is one design that can be infinitely adapted – use fur, felt or neoprene in place of leather and adjust the template to make a case for a phone, a tablet or an e-book.

You will need:

_ Leather jacket, lined (make sure the back is large enough to cover the laptop twice over)
_ A button
_ Scissors or leather shears
_ Sewing machine
_ Needle and thread

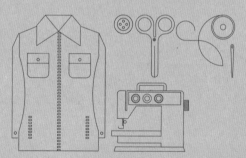

1_ Cut the entire back out of the jacket
   and lay it on a flat surface.

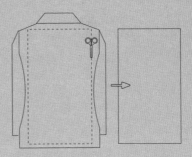

2_ Position the laptop on the leather and
   fold the leather so that the computer is
   sandwiched between two layers. Mark
   the size, allowing for an extra 2.5 cm
   all around the edge. If there is enough
   leather to include a cover flap as well
   add this to the measurements. Mark
   where the folds occur.

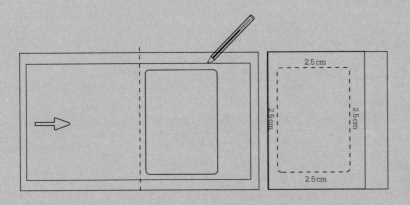

3_ Cut out the oblong shape as measured.
Use the leather piece as a template to
cut a section of the lining to the same
measurements, minus the flap. For
extra padding also add a layer of quilt
batting between the leather and the
lining – this should be the same size
less a centimetre or so on the sides.

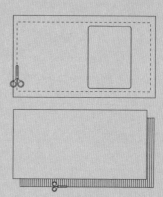

4_ Fold the leather into an envelope form,
right sides together. Snip the corners
off and sew using strong thread and,
if using a machine, the dedicated
settings and needle for sewing leather.

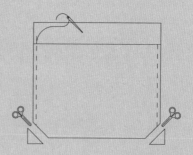

5_ Sew the lining pocket separately. Wrap
the batting around the lining and fold
the top edges of the lining in a hem to
secure, pin and sew into place.

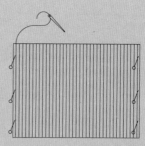

6_ Turn the leather pocket the right way out and sew the button onto the front where it will either slot through a button hole slit that you can make on the flap if there is one or it can be used to fasten a string around the case, like a manila envelope.

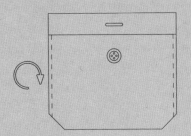

7_ If using a string, cut a long length of leather from one of the sleeves left over from the jacket and fasten it to the back of the cover in the centre, using a small square of leather to hold it in place. First sew around the edge of the square and then across it in an X shape.

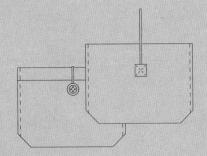

8_ Slip the lining into the leather pocket, pushing down the corners, and stitch it into place around the top edge, through all the layers.

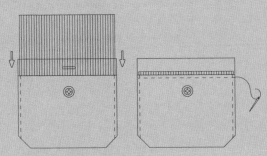

Joomi Lim
Mixology

Joomi Lim and Xavier Ricolfi launched their first collection of jewelry in 2009 with a range that mixes Lim's feminine design leanings with Ricolfi's industrial training through the use of unusual materials, finishes and technologies, from titanium plating to salvaging and reworking vintage items. The New York pair, who originally hail from Seoul and Paris respectively, are partners in life as well as work.

In the Mixology Collection, Lim combines vintage necklaces paired with spike charms and fringes. Inspired by the vibrant colour palettes found in Navajo Native American culture, each necklace is handmade.

Design example

Kotik Design
Precious metal

For Israeli designer Yoav Kotik, bottle tops and drink cans are not so much a cheap source of colourful metal that would otherwise go to waste, but rather intriguing and precious relics from different cultures filled with vast potential, and layered with history and meaning. Collecting them from around the world and treating each find with unprecedented care and attention, dusting each one off as if it were indeed a valuable treasure, Kotik and his team remodel their materials into jewelry.

Kotik's designs are highly considered and meticulously crafted and the results stand apart from other bottle-top creations, showing that it's not just the materials but the methods that really have the power to make a difference in this market.

Tamasyn Gambell
Recycled scarves

At her studio in London, textile print designer Tamasyn Gambell holds an ever-evolving collection of reclaimed scarves, sourced from a textile recycling plant near Nottingham. Using them as base canvases, Gambell overprints them with her own designs – the old and new patterns merging in intersecting graphic layers.

The recycled range is just one part of Gambell's eco-conscious print business, in which her Art Deco-inspired, bold and colourful patterns also adorn scarves newly woven and dyed in India by a cooperative of skilled women. The welfare project provides education, housing and healthcare for the communities. Gambell, who in the past has designed for Sonia Rykiel, Louis Vuitton and H&M among others, set up her own label in 2008. It was partly to allow her creative freedom, and partly with a view to taking a more responsible approach to producing luxury products. All aspects of the scarves' production and lifecycle, from the seaweed binder used in the screenprinting to the recycled packaging, are duly considered to ensure minimal environmental impact.

Design example
Bridget Harvey
Slow design

London-based Bridget Harvey uses wood off-cuts in combination with traditional textile techniques to create original, sustainable jewelry. Describing her methods and philosophy as fitting within a framework of "slow design and making", Harvey prioritizes environmentally sound materials. Her thoughtful, if necessarily time-consuming, process takes into account the potential use of every piece and its post-consumer options as well as the individual characteristics and pattern of each material and piece of wood used.

Harvey's manifesto stipulates the need to involve material manufacturers and suppliers in the design process alongside customers, and to give the same priority to the "thinking" as the "doing" stages.

-- Boyz in the snood --

Snood. It's not just a great word, but also a useful garment. A multi-functional marvel of minimalism, this tubular neck scarf can be worn around the neck as a scarf or with the back section pulled up as a hood. The word itself was first recorded some time around 725 and the snood was also widely used in the Middle Ages, before moving in and out of fashion over the centuries and eventually achieving fame and immortality as the preferred headwear of Grace Jones. Although traditionally a feminine look, the snood has made the leap into menswear with even some of the more conservative labels including them in their collections. Make a 21st-century snood with a large, tubular section cut from another large garment such as an oversized T, a sweater or the bottom of a cotton skirt or large top (hemmed).

-- Hood wink --

Depending on how it is worn, a good hood can suggest mystery, intrigue and drama, as well as warmth and wet-weather preparedness. An elegant drape of fine wool, perhaps lined with silk, looks great tucked under an evening jacket, while a double-layer jersey cotton hood works well with a sweater or anorak for casual lounging. Easy to make, a pattern for a stand-alone hood comprises just two pieces – one for each side of the head. It can be traced from an existing garment or drawn freehand and the pieces can be lined before sewing them together. For waterproof options you could try the plastic bag fabric, (see the step-by-step on pages 134–135) bubblewrap, an old shower curtain or oilcloth.

-- Keenly felt --

Industrial wool felt competes keenly with lycra as the superhero of fabrics. Strong, thick and highly resilient, it saves the day in all manner of situations as insulation, soundproofing and as a seal. It keeps its shape with little wear and tear over decades, and it can be cut painlessly with a clean edge, without ever unravelling or fraying. As well as its incredible insulating properties, it also has vibration-damping powers and amazing wicking capabilities. What could be more perfect, then, for making a pair of slippers? There are a number of designs and templates available that are relatively easy to make, from a single piece of felt folded over the foot and stitched in place, to more complicated patterns involving around three pieces per foot.

-- Learn the ropes --

Rope belts and jewelry can lend an edge to an otherwise delicate or refined look, and are a regular fixture of the wave of nautical fashion that comes and goes on an annual basis every spring. But while many a major fashion brand and designer have brought out some stunning statement examples over the years, homemade versions can look as good if not better. Curtain tie-backs, conveniently, are very often made of the same luxury rope used by the fashion houses and, at under a tenner (or swiped from the sitting room), are a lot cheaper. For a simple but beautiful necklace loop two different-coloured ties together and knot at the centre, but infinite versions can be made with the help of a sailing or climbing manual of professional knots and the addition of a beautiful clasp or buckle.

-- Shades of hope --

So you got fired, your team lost, you dropped out of college years ago, or maybe you just don't like the logo anymore – one way or another you don't want to pledge allegiance to the brand on your baseball cap a moment longer. Instead of ditching the whole hat, however, better just to downsize it to an infinitely cooler sun visor and relish the satisfaction of cutting up that logo at the same time. Cut the fabric so that there is a little extra above the headband, fold over the edge and glue it for a neat finish.

-- Sheepish postscript --
A small note about the tip opposite: there is in fact one thing that is more perfect from which to craft a pair of slippers than super industrial fantastic felt – a sheepskin rug. Leather side out, work to the same patterns as are available for a felt slipper, possibly extending the ankle up for an in-house Ugg boot effort.

STEP-BY-STEP

Homemade earmuffs

Chester Greenwood was 15 years old when he invented earmuffs in 1873.
As the story goes, he was frustrated at trying to wrap his head in a scratchy
scarf to keep his ears warm while iceskating, so he made two ear-shaped loops
out of wire and took them to his grandmother to make into something soft and
wearable. His company, Greenwood's Champion Ear Protectors, was established not
long after and he made his fortune supplying ear protectors to soldiers in the First
World War. His hometown, Farmington, Maine, is now the earmuff capital of the
world. (For junior upcyclers, this pattern can also make use of stuffed toys and
teddy bear heads in place of round ear pads.)

You will need:

_ Wire coat hanger
_ Scrap fabric (thick, furry, warm)
_ Cotton wool or other stuffing
_ Wire cutters
_ Scissors
_ CD (or similar sized round object
  for a template)
_ Tape measure
_ Knitting needle or chopstick
_ Sewing machine
_ Needle and thread for hand-finishing

1_ Cut the coat hanger using the wire
   cutters to give you one long strip.

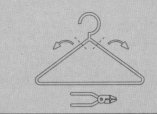

2_ Bend the wire into your base shape,
   incorporating a large round loop either
   side of a head-shaped bend. Try it on
   and adjust to give a comfortable fit.

3_ Measure the central band of wire
and, adding a few centimetres to the
length, cut a strip of fabric about 8 cm
in width.

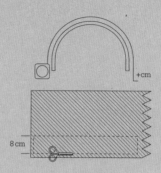

8 cm

4_ Sew this strip (right sides together)
into a long tube and turn it back the
right way.

5_ Using the CD as a template, mark
and cut out four circles of the fabric.
Pin two circles right sides together
and sew around the edges, leaving
an opening at the top of around 7 cm.
Repeat with the other two circles.

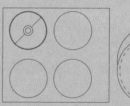

6_ Turn the circular ear pads the right
way out and stuff them until firm.

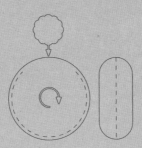

7_ Carefully insert the fabric pieces onto
the wire. Stuff the fabric that goes over
the head, using a knitting needle or
chopstick to push the stuffing along.

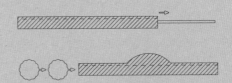

8_ Tuck the ends of the centre strip into
the openings at the top of the ear
pieces and hand-stitch them closed.

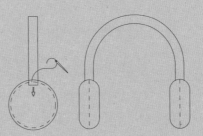

Design example
Hetty Rose
Kimono collection
Hetty Rose bespoke shoes are
handmade using reclaimed,
recycled and vintage materials:
Exquisite vintage Japanese silk
kimono fabrics are a favourite
for their rich colours and
patterns loaded with meaning.
Directly sourced from Japan by
the label's creator, Henrietta
Rose Samuels, the textiles are
recrafted into uppers and paired
with wooden heels and recycled
leather soles, all individually
hand-crafted in Chelmsford.

Design example
Camila Labra
Botas dacca
Wearing plastic bags as footwear is usually reserved for those dodgy situations that require it as a hygiene measure, but Chilean designer Camila Labra had other ideas when she chose material made from fused plastic bags to create a range of sustainable boots.

Crisp, colourful and right on the eco-fashion pulse, she found a global market for her project, Dacca, when she posted it on the internet in 2008. Dacca ceased trading when Labra (aged just 23 at the time) took up a research position in materials.

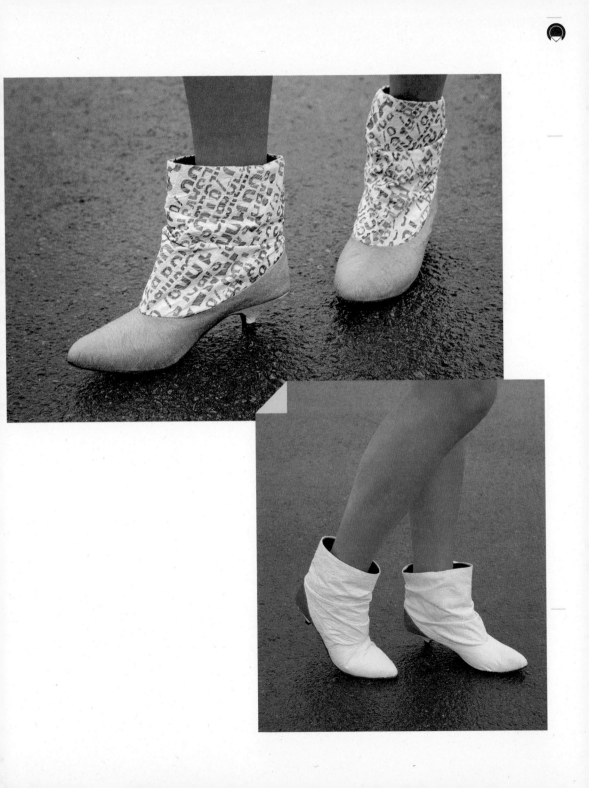

STEP-BY-STEP

Stay in the shade

Give a pair of heels and a handbag a paint job to give them a fresh lease of life and dance into a new era. Or into an old one – the mid-1980s do a nice line in inspiration here. Dual tones and airbrushed effects are particularly evocative of disco days – use neon on black for an authentic luxe trash punk look, but plain shades will also be effective and a lick (or a spray) of paint can just as easily be used to refresh rather than reinvent a design, especially in the case of scuffed patent leather.

You will need:

_ Shoes/handbag/plastic bangles
  to be painted
_ Newspaper

_ Stripper
_ Masking tape
_ Spray paint for plastic or leather

1_ Lay out the newspaper in a well-ventilated space.
2_ Rub the stripper over the handbag to clean it and remove any oils or polish that might mar the finish of the new paint.
3_ Cover any areas that you are not painting with masking tape.
4_ Pack the insides of the handbag with newspaper.
5_ Shake the can and, holding it vertically, spray 20–30 cm away from the handbag in a slow sweeping motion. It is best to build up the colour gradually to prevent drips forming and to create a more even finish.
6_ Leave to dry for 1 to 2 hours before applying a second coat. If adding a second colour, let the first coat dry completely before you apply the second.
7_ When you have finished applying the paint and all the layers are dry remove the masking tape and paper.

1_

2_

3_

4_

5_

6_

1-2 hrs

7_

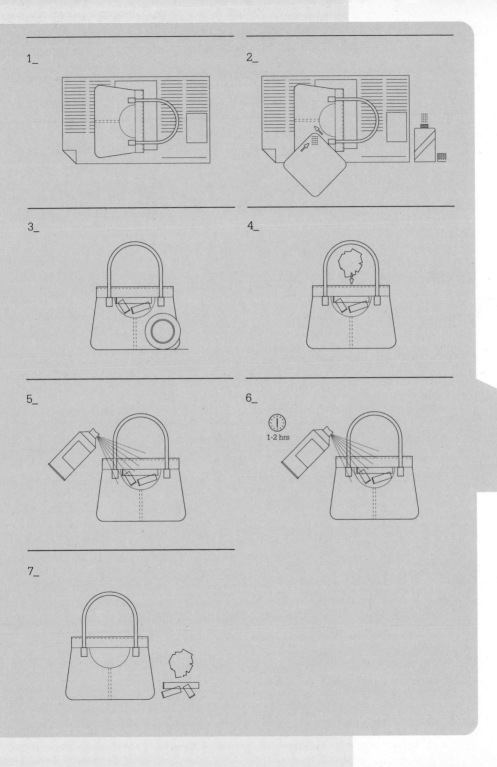

Design example
Freitag
Tarpaulin accessories

Swiss luggage company Freitag was born in 1993 when two brothers, both graphic designers, were on the lookout for a heavy duty messenger bag that would withstand the wind and rain and in which they could carry their designs around Zurich by bike. Inspired by the brightly coloured lorries that passed their apartment on a daily basis, they duly found some old truck tarpaulin and cut their own bags from it. They used some old car seatbelt webbing for the straps and a bicycle inner tube for the edging.

Pleased enough with the results to start their own company, they called it Freitag – not, as is popularly assumed in English-speaking countries, because they always use tarp from freight lorries, and not, as German-speaking customers might believe, because they had their epiphany idea on a Friday. It's just their surname. Markus and Daniel Freitag developed the design into an original line that would quickly include more than 40 models and bag types, before they added seasonal collections and fashion lines. All products still adhere to the original ethos of remaking and they are all still made in Switzerland.

Design example
Freitag
Tarpaulin accessories

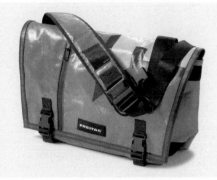

Design example
Diana Eng
Fortune cookie coin purse
Each Fortune Cookie Coin Purse made by designer and innovator Diana Eng is marked with a laser-etched ID number which can be used as a key to discover and track its origin. Made in the US from recycled leather, the purses may be fashioned from pre-consumer scraps from a high-end designer furniture company or from remnant leather from the garment district. Since the coin purse pattern is so small, clean areas of pelt can be salvaged from samples that might be too marked or soiled for most other uses. Like real fortune cookies, the Fortune Cookie Coin Purses contain a printed fortune inside.

-- Sole trader --

The first step any well-heeled environmentally conscious consumer needs to take is to invest in a good pair of shoes that are made to last. The second is to look after them and the third is to have them repaired as they eventually do start showing wear and tear. Although resoling a shoe with leather is a professional task and worth visiting a shoemaker or cobbler, it's quite a straightforward job to add a new sole to old shoes using rubber or foam, which might be salvaged from floor mats or elsewhere. Necessary tools include extremely strong glue, a sharp knife to cut around the sole (which you can do after attaching it to the shoe) and a sander (optional) to file down the edges at the end.

-- Waisting time --

A leather watch strap also makes a brilliant belt. Don't worry, it doesn't mean you have to diet until you're the size of an anorexic mouse. Add a metal link loop to each strap, to which the ends of a silk scarf can be knotted, leaving a silk belt in the space where the watch face was.

-- Packing muscle --

The early 20th century was a golden age of travel, when steam trains, cruiseliners, aeroplanes and motorcars ushered in an exciting new world of exploration and mass tourism. And it was fully accessorized with a golden age of luggage. Boxy monogrammed suitcases and trunks, complete with leather straps, reinforced corners and chunky hardware tell nostalgic stories of glamour, adventure and wanderlust in a way that a black nylon expandable trolley might not. Sadly, bearing in mind that practicality is paramount when travelling, an antique suitcase rarely meets the demands of the modern nomad and it can be a mission (and an expensive one) to find cases in good enough nick. Even then, the security features are invariably lacking compared to new designs. But where there's a will there is usually a way: mouldy tattered linings can be replaced, clasps and straps can be fixed-up or exchanged entirely. And for the contemporary globetrotter whose budget might not extend to the (more authentic) porter, a good repair shop may even be able to fit it with a retractable trolley handle and castors.

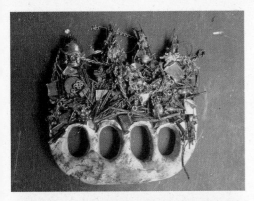

Design example

Glovedup Gloves
Fingerless gloves

Seeing beyond the traditional role of gloves as woolly winter hand-warmers, Laura Shepherd carved a happy niche for herself as a pioneer of contemporary, bespoke and mainly fingerless gloves – spectacular gloves for stars on stage, whimsical and wonderful gloves for style and fashion editorials and all manner of other gloves that essentially "didn't exist before". Frequently working with found materials and upcycled leather to create her popular one-of-a-kind creations, including puffed-sleeved gloves, driving gloves and knuckle-warmers, Shepherd also has fingers in other pies: epaulettes, recycled plastic bag hand-fans and tiaras to name a few.

STEP-BY-STEP

Duct tales

Duct tape is amazing. Originally invented in 1942 during the Second World War, the water-resistant super strong fabric-backed tape was used to seal ammunition cases before people began to cotton on to its usefulness and used it to fix up everything from firearms to aeroplanes. Still a firm favourite at NASA (whose astronauts famously used it to save the day on the Apollo 13 space mission in 1970), with a couple of rolls it is possible to make or mend almost anything. The all-time classic hack, and possibly the most universally useful, has to be the duct-tape wallet. This design is highly customizable, so let rip with all the different colours and widths of tape available.

You will need:

_ Duct tape
_ Stanley knife
_ Ruler
_ Clear plastic sheet for
  ID card window (optional)

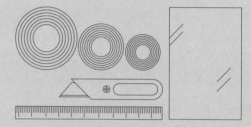

1_ Begin by making a large sheet of duct tape "fabric", around 18 x 22 cm. To do this, rip two 22 cm strips of tape from the roll. Place the first sticky side up before laying the second, sticky side down, half way over the first strip lengthways. Fold up the first strip to meet (but not overlap) the second strip. Flip the fabric over and add a third strip to cover the remaining sticky part of the second strip. Flip again, add a strip and so on until you get the right size. Fold over the last edge. The key throughout is to try to keep the layers of tape to a minimum for ease of folding later on.

2_ Trim the side edges and fold the fabric in half (with the tape running horizontally). Cut two narrow strips of tape and use these to tape the sides closed. You should now have a long pocket for bank notes.

3_ Make two more sheets of fabric, this time around 9 x 10 cm. These will be used to make the card pockets. Fold 3 cm over on both sheets, then tape the two pieces together, placing them so that one sits a little lower than the other.

4_ Tape the edges of the pockets closed and then fix the whole piece to the large pocket.

5_ Cut the plastic sheet to a slightly bigger size than your ID card and tape a narrow frame across the top edge.

6_ Tape the sides and the bottom into the wallet to make another pocket.

7_ Fold the wallet in half horizontally. You can stop there or carry on and customize the design to add a coin purse, more pockets or graphics.

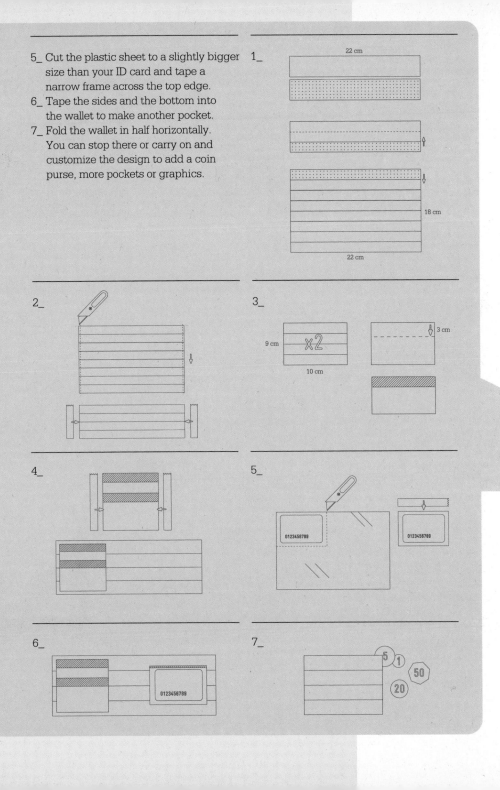

Design example
Worn Again
Eurostar uniforms

Worn Again is a British company that works with global brands to upcycle their textiles waste into new products. Established in 2005, its input has seen McDonald's commit to a long-term aim of achieving 100% closed loop textiles and Royal Mail prototype a storm sack from the heavy duty jackets worn on delivery rounds.

Working with cross channel rail company Eurostar, Worn Again commissioned London-based designer Benjamin Shine to create a new bag for train managers using decommissioned staff uniforms and train-seat covers. After much consultation with Eurostar staff about their specific requirements, the resulting bag incorporates fabric from staff raincoats, lining from suit jackets and foam from antimacassars. It is expressly designed to accommodate specialist equipment and materials such as a train manager's book, a torch and stamps. High visibility vests are stored at the base of the bag.

-- Nice buns --

For an endless supply of elastic hair ties and headbands, cut sections across the legs of an old pair of tights or stockings. Pull the bands taut so the edges will furl up of their own accord, preventing any fraying and stopping the bands from looking like a section of old hosiery at the same time. This also works with any jersey fabric that doesn't need hemming – for instance, offcuts from a pair of leggings or a T-shirt.

-- Out on a limb --

As dancers, goths and harajuku girls already well know, leg- and arm-warmers are a versatile accessory as well as a practical one. They are also a perfect repurpose for those spare sleeves from a sweater hack. Just cut the knitted tubes to the desired length (with a woollen garment consider felting the sleeves first in order to get the right size and to be able to cut without fraying), then turn over a hem on the end where the shoulder once was, also including a little elastic. If using them as arm-warmers, consider adding holes for the thumbs.

-- Headers and footers --

If the idea is just to get ahead, get a hat by all means. But to create an aura of intrigue and wonder, while still reaching the upper echelons of the vertical fashion scales, get a fascinator. Better still, make one. Fascinators, the elaborate headpieces commonly seen giving their jaunty angles on coiffed heads at formal occasions such as the races, polo matches or weddings, have come back into fashion in recent years – a resurgence that owes as much to a renewed interest in burlesque as to influential fascinator ambassadors in the royal family. Building an elegant and impressive headpiece at home isn't complicated even for amateur milliners. First select a base (this can be a barrette, a plain thin headband or a hair comb) and cover it with a sturdy fabric such as felt or interfacing a little larger than the clip or comb and strong enough to support the weight of the end design. Either glue the fabric to the clip using a strong glue or stitch it on by hand and then decorate the surface. Feathers, a veil of tulle, silk flowers and beads have all made for fascinating cocktail hats, as have lobsters, bunny ears, telephones and shoes.

Design example
Christian Louboutin
Eco-trash

The heel heights may vary slightly (though rarely dipping lower than 12 cm) and styles and fashions run the gamut from a demure black pump through to an outrageous neon spaghetti junction of straps, but the unmistakable flash of a glossy red sole will forever give away a pair of Christian Louboutin shoes. This singular trademark feature, which saw the Parisian designer create a firm foothold for stilettos throughout the 1990s and 2000s, as well as an international fanbase and network of stores, initially came about by accident. According to his US trademark application, Louboutin felt that his designs were lacking a vital energy. "So I applied red nail polish to the sole of a shoe. This was such a success that it became a permanent fixture."

Much later in 2010 Louboutin would experiment with another remaking approach: the Eco-Trash pump. Made using recycled waste materials (with leopard print accents), the shoe was intended to be the height (15 cm no less) of eco-chic.

-- Swish buckling adventure --

Buckles can be salvaged and reused from old belts, bags and straps, customized or entirely homemade. A D-ring-style belt buckle, in particular, allows for a great deal of improvisation: a couple of curtain rings, old jewelry or perhaps a spare knuckle duster will do. Loop and secure one end of the belt around the rings, as with haberdashery equivalents.

-- Playing with food --

Carmen Miranda's fruit hat notwithstanding, a quick raid of the kitchen ought to provide ample inspiration for a resourceful accessorizer. Whip up a feast of simple, natural and beautiful jewelry using seeds from fruit – pumpkin, melons and chirilla seeds, dried, painted or left natural and varnished – strung on a fine string or chain, set into a brooch or made into earrings. Alternatively, a bracelet or necklace of colourful hard candies can be a sweet addition to an outfit, while also ensuring a convenient snack option for later. Meanwhile, food packaging, aluminium foil and cling film will become unrecognizable when made into beads (cut it into strips and roll it). Fruit nets, with a few snips and tucks, will provide a hat or a fascinator with a veil, and forks and spoons can be craftily bent into bracelets that look good enough to eat with.

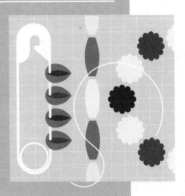

-- Geta life --

The Geta is a traditional Japanese wooden shoe that looks a little like a cross between a flip-flop and a clog and is just as satisfyingly clackity and comfortable to wear. Easy to make with only the most basic of woodworking skills, each shoe consists of a single-piece wooden sole and two risers across the bottom, one under the heel, the other beneath the centre of the foot. Traditionally hand-crafted from paulownia wood, any spare timber will do as long as it can be sanded smooth enough so as not to cause splinters. The upper part of the shoe should be made of strong, thin rope or folded fabric which runs from the side of the Geta over the foot and is threaded through to the sole and secured between the toes. Wear with (homemade) split-toed white socks.

CHILDREN AND PETS

Bags, sweaters, balaclavas, fancy dress, pinafores, aprons, T-shirts, bibs, hats, blouses and skirts

-- Sock summit --

Although "balaclava" is surely such a brilliant word that nobody
would need an alternative descriptor, someone has come up with one
all the same. Understandably, not many people use the somewhat
less glamorous-sounding word headsock, but while the mysterious
balaclava, named after the town of the same name in Crimea, Ukraine,
reveals nothing about its knitted close-fitting entire-head-covering
function, the more literal headsock does rather give the game away.
It might also provide a little remaking inspiration. Large men's silk
socks will cut down beautifully for a baby balaclava, keeping a little
head warm in winter, while also making soft scratchproof protectors
for itchy eczema-prone babas. The functional part here is the heel,
so cut away the sock across the ball of the foot and at the ankle.
Make sure there is enough give in the fabric so that it won't be too tight.

-- Honey, I shrunk the kids --

Felted woollen sweaters can be upcycled into all manner of warm and
wonderful children's clothes, but when a favourite and/or expensive
sweater is miniaturized accidentally it's easy to lose perspective, and
sometimes it's difficult to take the scissors to it. The best idea in this
case is often to turn it into a sweet child's cardigan by making a single
cut up the centre and adding buttons and button loops to fasten it.
In this form, any stiffness resulting from the shrinkage doesn't matter
so much as it won't be pulled on over the head, but the design will
largely stay intact, bringing back memories every time it's worn by
your mini-me.

-- Mini keeper --

The tiny onesies that make up so much of the first six months
of parenthood are shockingly shortlived. Babies have a habit of
outgrowing their babygrows faster than seems polite, frankly, given all
the work and generosity of friends and relatives involved in stockpiling
them prior to their arrival. But they can't be blamed, they're only little
(ish). Instead (and if no more arrivals are expected in the near future)
upcycle the onesies into new garments: cut off the bottom, keeping the
length as long as possible to make a T-shirt which should last a few
more months at least. Add a ruffle at the bottom to make it longer still,
and shorten the sleeves if they are too tight at the cuffs.

Design example
Minna
Children's collection

Minna Hepburn began producing children's clothing in 2009, inspired by her own daughter Kristiina, who wanted to wear the designs she saw her mother making for her grown-up range of dresses. Staying away from the antique lace she had used to build up her label of womenswear and bridal collections, this time the dresses would be made entirely from leftover and end-of-roll textiles, and feature playful details and hand embellishments.

Design example
Pamoyo
Kings and queens
Led by designer Cecilia Palmer, Berlin-based Pamoyo is an ethical and environmentally sound fashion label set up in 2008. Palmer works alongside an ever-increasing team of collaborators and all of Pamoyo's designs are shared under a Creative Commons licence which means they are freely available and open to infinite variations by customization or remaking. Palmer's aim is that every collection should be based around a new artistic invention or social statement as opposed to following fashion trends and all the pieces are created by upcycling locally sourced vintage garments, combining them with organic, fairtrade cotton. Swedish-born Berliner Mika Modiggård was responsible for Pamoyo's first collection of children's clothing in 2010. Called "Kings and Queens", it was inspired by urban ghetto culture, hip hop music and 1990s streetwear.

-- Pop psychology --

Save any surplus bubblewrap packaging for a rainy day. Softer and more comfortable than many waterproof materials (oilcloth and tarps can be quite stiff), bubblewrap has the added advantage of interactivity – popping the little bubbles is well known to provide great relief from boredom and stress for children and parents alike. Use larger sheets to make raincapes and smaller pieces for sou'wester-style hats and hoods. Don't worry about linings, but use a colourful bias binding to edge the pieces before stitching them together.

-- Slumber jacket --

Parents with the urge to wrap up their little ones in cotton wool might think first about upcycling an old sleeping bag for the job instead. Their lightweight but insulated construction is well suited for cocoon-like clothes for cold weather, often waterproof and sometimes even fully equipped with a readymade hood. In the case of the latter, the simplest garment to make might be a slip-on, hooded, padded gilet, but sleeves can be added, too, while tiny trousers and house slippers are other ways to keep tots toasty.

-- Eco-warrior --

Recycling schemes for PET bottles often forget one of the best reuses there is: body armour. With bottles of every size and shape under the sun now available, it should be possible to construct a suit of armour to match any era, character and child around. Large, round 5-litre bottles can be cut to make effective helmets, while the standard 2.5-litre water bottles cut in half vertically will usually serve as excellent shin and arm guards. Collect as many bottles as possible before going to war on them with a Stanley knife and sketch out a rough design for the armour on paper first. Cut strips and overlap them to enable movement. Once the design has been worked out and arranged, make holes in the ends or corners of each "plate" before covering them with foil, paper, tape or paint. Be sure to round off any sharp corners and eliminate sharp edges (masking tape works well for this). Then using an elasticated thread lightly stitch each one in place through the holes. Simple, close-fitting, cotton, neutral-coloured top and bottoms (such as old pyjamas) work well. For accuracy, if the soldier-in-waiting is a patient soul, it's easiest to sew directly onto the garment while it's being worn. That way the joints are more likely to sit in the right place.

-- Woof top lounge --

Little paws need a rest from time to time on longer journeys, so turn an old sweatshirt or woollen sweater into a new tote bag in which more petite pooches can be delightfully transported around town. Following the steps on pages 180–81 to turn a T-shirt into a shopper, just add an opening in the side for headspace and a lookout. If the sweatshirt originally had a hood, this can be refashioned to fit onto the side of the bag, so covering the opening if the dog is sleeping or providing it with a warm and cosy hood when looking out. The whole shebang will fold up small and fit inside another bag when not in use.

-- Education in life --

Any items of school uniform no longer needed or grown out of can be reincarnated for extra-curricular wear with a few simple adjustments. Turn girls' shirts into smart blouses by removing the collar and adding a bow detail or ruffles, or shorten a skirt and add a contrasting waistband or trim. Often changing the colour or adding a print or graphic design of some sort is all that is necessary to remove classroom connotations. School uniform shops, too, are often a source of cost-effective basics for customization, whether or not your children are on the assembly roll.

-- Catchall solution --

The perfect aeroplane-to-open-mouth landing takes some serious air traffic control sometimes, but as well as adding protection during messier mealtimes, it's worth mastering the very easy art of making a good bib from scratch if only because they make such excellent presents. The process is as simple as finding a good shape and tracing it onto the fabric to be upcycled – surplus shirts, old T-shirts and dishcloths are the ubiquitous choices, but for something waterproof cast around for an old oilcloth tablecloth, shower curtain or umbrella. The amount of fabric needed is minimal. Use an existing bib as a template and cut two pieces of fabric, the same or contrasting, and pin them right sides out together all around the edge. Sew as close to the edges as possible before finishing them with bias binding and a fastener such as a large popper or button.

<u>STEP-BY-STEP</u>

Jamming session

Getting little people into their pyjamas can be difficult at the best of times, but staying on top of the situation when also faced with accelerating growth rates can be expensive too. While the idea of whizzing up a homemade nightie before bedtime might sound like something reserved only for domestic gods and goddesses of the highest order, once a little helper or two have been engaged in the task, and given a good stockpile of raw material in the form of daddy's old shirts, T-shirts and perhaps the odd pillowcase, it's a 20-minute task at most and, with a bit of practice, less. And at the end of it the mini models can strut the sleepy catwalk straight to bed.

1. T-shirt nightdress

You will need:
_ T-shirt
_ Scissors
_ Pins
_ Chalk pencil
_ Bias binding, ribbon or cord
_ Tape measure
_ Needle and thread

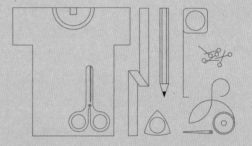

1_ Measure how long you want the nightdress to be on the child and mark this on the T-shirt. The existing hem will be the hem on the finished dress. Cut along the line to form a tube.

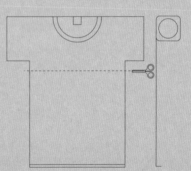

2_ Narrow the tube if necessary by cutting up the sides. Pin the cut edges, right sides together, and sew to make a new seam.

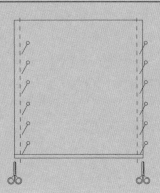

3_ Using a sleeveless item or sweater, trace two armholes at the top corners or draw a J shape freehand. For this design – which has shoulder ties – the armhole openings won't reach the top of the shoulders. The top of the tube is really the height of the neckline. Cut out the armholes.

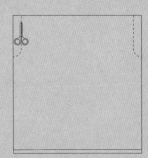

4_ Use bias binding to finish the edges of the armholes, extending it up to form string straps that are long enough to tie in bows above the shoulder. Measure, press and pin the binding in place before sewing.

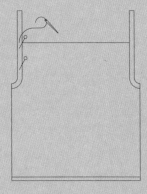

5_ Use another couple of strips of binding
to finish the neck opening at the front
and back. You might want to gather
and hem the neckline first using a long
running stitch before binding it with
a top stitch. This will make a better
fit and create a more professional-
looking finish.

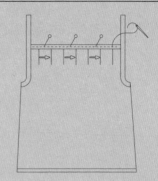

6_ Put the dress on the child and tie the
shoulder straps before trimming off any
excess from the straps and sending
her to bed.

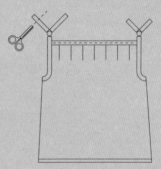

7_ On another night, continue the project
by decorating the nightie using
appliqué.

For an even faster turnaround, rather than
using the binding, hem the neckline and
armholes and add a thin cord or ribbon
to make the straps. Matching pieces
of just about the right length can often
be salvaged from posh shopping bag
handles. This design can also be adapted
to make a girl's pyjama top by making it
a bit shorter.

2. T-shirt pyjama bottoms

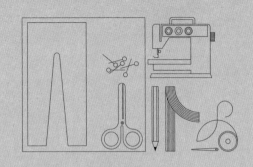

You will need:
- _ T-shirt or any salvaged fabric
- _ Pyjama bottoms
- _ Scissors
- _ Pins
- _ Needle and thread
- _ Chalk pencil
- _ Sewing machine
- _ Elastic

Making mini pyjama bottoms by tracing around an existing pair takes hardly anytime at all, while the materials needed just include some cotton or flannel salvaged from extra large old T-shirts, shirts or thin towels and some elastic. This is an ingenious way to use up patterned children's pillowcases, sheets and duvet covers.

1_ Take the fabric and fold it lengthwise selvedge to selvedge. Then fold the selvedges separately back towards the centre fold to give a sort of concertina effect, making sure the folded edges are matched up.

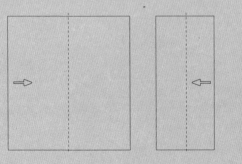

2_ Fold the pyjama bottoms you're using
as a pattern in half and line up the
straight side with the folds of your
fabric. Trace around the bottoms,
adding a couple of centimetres to
the vertical edges, the hem and
the waistband, remembering to
compensate for the elastic waist.

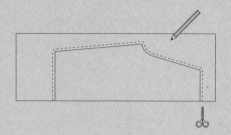

3_ Cut out the pieces with the fabric still
stacked. You should have two Grecian
vase-shaped pieces.

4_ Lay the cut pieces right sides together
and pin and sew along the curved
sections (the crotch seams).

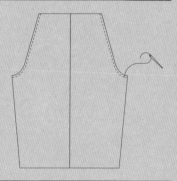

5_ Line up the front centre and back
centre seams so they match and pin
and sew down the leg seams.

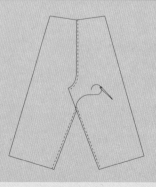

6_ Make a casing for the elastic
   waistband by folding over the top
   edge of the bottoms by about 2 cm.
   Pin and sew all the way around.
   Leave an opening at the centre seam
   to insert the elastic. You can feed it
   through using a safety pin. It's best to
   do a fitting at this stage to make sure
   the elastic is the right length. Once
   you've done this then you can stitch it
   together. You can also use a drawstring
   instead of elastic.

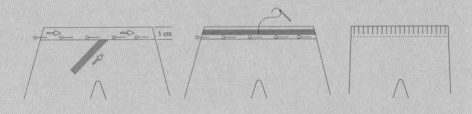

7_ Turn the pyjama bottoms right side out
   and hem the legs. Jammin'.

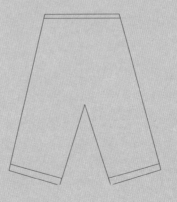

Design example

Stella Neptune
Moth patches

Thrift addict Eva Kisevalter
was a DJ, spinning vinyl by
her dedicated DJ name Stella
Neptune, before she became a
designer. The name stuck when
the tune changed and her career
took an entirely new direction
into an environmentally sound
clothing line. Today, Stella
Neptune stands instead for
recycled cashmere garments,
sourced, screenprinted and
appliquéd all within a 10-mile
radius of her Los Angeles studio.
Specializing in moth patches
to cover the random patterns
of holes left on sweaters
by picnicking moths, Stella
Neptune also does a lovely line in
sweaters and miniature panelled
cashmere skirts for children.

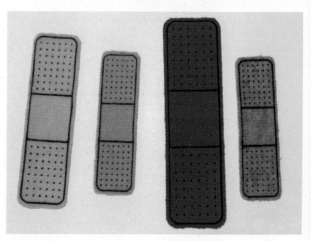

-- Walking wardrobe --

In the eyes of an imaginative remaker, the entire house, garage, junk yard or thrift store is just one big dressing-up box. As anyone who works in a theatre or film costume and set department will know, an ability to visualize and improvise are the most useful skills on the job, and this applies as much to turning a baby into a Dalmation puppy for Halloween as it does to transforming a chiwawa into a banana for a walk in the Harujuku hills. Some basics:

- Hats are a fundamental starting-point for many costumes. Adjust grown-up millinery to fit little heads with the addition of lots of cotton wool or cut up a sponge and fix small pieces around the inside rim.
- Four wire coat hangers plus two pairs of coloured tights are a basic equation for butterfly or insect wings.
- A battered black umbrella can be deconstructed and reconstructed into a pair of brilliant bat wings.
- Angel wings, however, require feathers (which can be homemade from paper) and a single large piece of stiff but lightweight card (or two pieces, for independent wings). Angels or insects can affix their wings directly to the rest of their outfit or to a harness using a few strong stitches or temporary fastenings such as hooks or velcro.
- A lot of surplus fake fur of any colour will clearly make a cuddly mini monster, but it's still possible to make a massive difference with a few centimetres of the stuff: the film careers of Tom Selleck or Burt Reynolds should provide ample inspiration.
- Huge cardboard boxes such as those used in house moves or for new appliances often make excellent vehicles, buildings and robots, with the basic addition of some wheels, windows and a paint job accordingly. Often coming fully equipped with big chunks of polystyrene, these can be put to good use when accessorizing.
- Dustbin and saucepan lids traditionally make the best shields, with minimum adaptation to match the rest of the outfit.
- When it comes to animal antics, the possibilities are as endless as the millions of species of remarkable fauna on the planet. But keeping a small stash of ears and tails is never a bad idea. Adding spots, stripes or other markings to a toddler's onesie takes a matter of minutes.
- The Michelin Man costume is always a hit for sleepovers. A duvet, tied in sections with a few pieces of string, will do the job nicely. Sleeping bags make great caterpillars.

Clothkits
Mailorder dressmaking

Etched onto the memories of a whole generation, Clothkits' bold, bright geometric patterns evoke a world of nostalgia for homespun 1970s liberal living. The phenomenally successful British brand, founded in 1969 by designer Anne Kennedy at her kitchen table, sold simple-to-follow, very distinctive sew-your-own kits, which she made by printing dressmaking pieces directly onto coloured fabric. Kennedy marketed the kits with the help of her children, who modelled the final results.

Patterns for dresses, dungarees and skirts (with matching knickers) were dispatched by the thousand. At its peak, the Lewes-based company employed more than 400 people and was selling to 44 countries worldwide. Sew-your-own kits formed the core of the business, supplemented by knitwear.

The company ran into difficulties in the late 1980s when incoming computerization made things more complicated for Kennedy. Her market had also dwindled as more women were going out to work and sewing less. Clothkits was sold and by 1991 it had been made dormant.

Some 17 years later, in 2008, artist and one-time wearer of Clothkits originals, Kay Mawer, bought the brand and relaunched it. Continuing the mission to produce kit clothing as per the original concept, and still maintaining its much-loved retro hippie feel, Mawer also organized collaborations with contemporary artists and designers including screenprinter Jane Foster, papercut artist Rob Ryan and People Will Always Need Plates.

DUNGAREES
Style 341

Dungarees are among the most practical garments for toddlers and Clothkits have designed a really simple pair with only two main pattern pieces sporting a delightful cat and mouse print. The kit includes one long leg pocket, one patch pocket and quick release clips. The kit is easy to make and a good introduction to Clothkits.

Fabric: 100% cotton, machine washable
Colours: RED with navy print
LILAC with turquoise print
GREEN with pine green print
RUST with navy print
Size: 18mths–2 years
Price: £2.60

DUNGAREES
Style 342

Fierce members of the cat family decorate four older children's dungarees. Included is a large bib pocket, one leg pocket and one smaller back pocket/patch. The fly zip is optional. Popular demand has persuaded us to re-introduce our 5–7 sizes.

Fabric: 100% cotton, machine washable
Colours: RED with navy print
LILAC with turquoise print
GREEN with pine green print
RUST with navy print
Size: 2–4   5–7
Price: £3.25 £3.95

Please order by colour in CAPITALS.

GREEN   RED

BABY SMOCK
Style 359

Sweet little smock and pants set in practical polyester/cotton. The smock is simple to make with only 2 main pattern pieces which can be simply gathered onto a neckband and worn open at the back. Alternatively the yoke can be shirred following our instructions (shirring elastic included) and the smock can be worn buttoned at the front.

Fabric: 67% polyester, 33% cotton
Colours: CREAM with pink and grey print
RED with rust and navy print
Size: 0–2
Price: £2.36

Please order by colour in CAPITALS.

CREAM baby smock & pants

RED baby smock & pants

RED baby smock and pants

GIRLS' SKIRT
Style 344

Pretty flared skirt and suntop with a sampler-inspired print. This is ideal for embroidery – see our brief attempt in red on the suntop which is trimmed with thick cotton laces to match the print colours. These cross over and tie at the back.

Fabric: 100% cotton, machine washable
Colours: RED, LILAC, RUST, WHITE
Size: 8–11
Price: £2.99

RUST skirt

NAVY T-shirt

WHITE skirt

WHITE   RED

LILAC   RUST   CREAM   RED

clothkits
SUMMER 1972

WINTER 1970–71   **clothkits**

Design example

Clothkits
Mailorder dressmaking

ROSE
Pinafore &
BROWN
hat (page 14)
ROSE
T-shirt &
socks
(page 3 & 4)

PINAFORE Style 493 ✂ ✳

The kit picture opposite will give you an idea of how easy it is to make this pretty and practical pinafore with its cheerful apple tree print. The dress has only one main piece and fastens with a zip at the back, baskets of apples decorate the patch pockets. The kit also includes a matching pinafore dress to fit our Rag doll "Cloth-Kitty" (see page 48-49) or most other 17" dolls. (Sorry, the doll's pinafore cannot be supplied separately).

See pages 2, 3 and 4 for matching T-shirts and socks and page 12 for sunhat. The skirt on page 29 shows the Buttercup colourway.

FABRIC: 100% cotton, machine washable.

COLOURS: (Swatch 3) Brown with ROSE print, AQUA with blue print, Natural with BUTTERCUP print, SAFARI with coffee print.

SIZE: 1-3   4-6
PRICE: £2.45   £2.75
Please order by colour in CAPITALS.

AQUA pinafore &
hat
CORNFLOWER T-shirt
& socks (page 3 & 4)

STEP-BY-STEP

Tote recall

In the war effort against the evil plastic carrier bag, the world's companies and corporations have rushed to supply consuming armies with a far more eco-friendly shopping weapon instead, the reusable fabric tote. This is all very well and good, but as the polyethylene pile under the sink starts to dwindle, another one – of long-handled fabric rectangles printed with slogans and logos and pictures of planets – is growing. And the inconvenient truth is that there are only so many reusable fabric totes one can realistically reuse at a time.

Unless, that is, the tote is reused as a dress. Dresses, unlike supermarket shopping bags, are something of which the world can surely never have too many. And this is true especially of very little ladies for whom making a mess of said dress is a ritual to be repeated several times a day.

You will need:

_ Fabric tote bag
_ Sewing machine
_ Thread
_ Scissors
_ Elastic
_ Poppers or other fasteners as preferred
_ Stitch unpick

_ Pins
_ Ruler
_ Chalk pencil
_ Iron

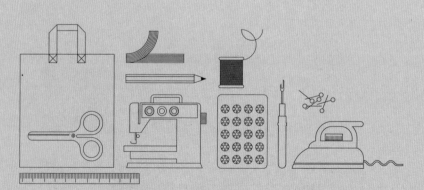

1_ Unpick the thread on one side and
   along the bottom of the bag and
   open it out flat.

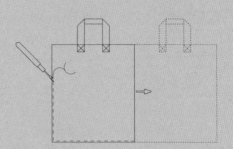

2_ Iron, pin and hem the raw edges.

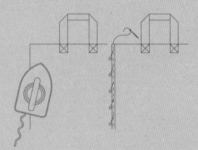

3_ Re-fold the fabric so that the handles
of the bag are positioned as shoulder
straps. The fabric at the front should
overlap by about 1 cm.

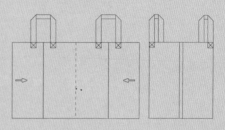

4_ Position the fastenings and mark the
fabric where they will go on both sides.
Poppers or hook-and-eye fastenings
are an easy choice, but buttons or a zip
will also work just as well.

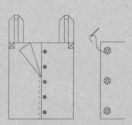

5_ Sew on the fastenings. Stage a fitting
for the dress at this point, if possible,
and measure and adjust the length of
the straps to fit. The straps can either
be shortened by cutting and resewing
or, if they are long enough to start with,
by simply cutting them at the top and
then tying them together in a bow.
Alternatively, you could cut the straps
off entirely and replace them with
ribbon ties at this stage.

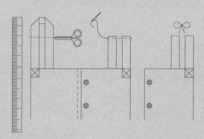

6_ Measure around the middle and cut
a length of elastic the same length.

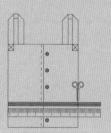

7_ Stitch the elastic in place, either round
the waist as in stage 6 or under the
bust as here.

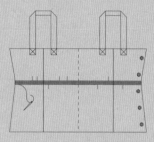

8_ Gather the middle section in to make a
secure and comfortable fit.

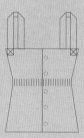

-- Room for inflation --

Letting out children's clothes was an art perfected during the Second World War, and Mrs Sew-and-Sew devoted whole pamphlets to the cause. As a rule, she said, one should always make and buy children's clothes slightly on the big side to start with, but although that will make the garments last longer, they will still need adjusting to fit. Better advice for modern parents is to buy and make clothes that leave generous turnings and hems to allow for easier enlargement when the time comes. Although every garment will suggest different opportunities and ideas, in most cases the garment to be let out should be completely unpicked from hem to underarm and along the sleeve seam until the whole garment can be opened out in one piece. The trick is then to add contrasting bands of material at the sides and the waist, while a new yoke can be made to lengthen a dress and let it out under the arms.

-- Split piece --

When a favourite dress has been grown out of and there's nobody immediately next in line for a hand-me-down, one way to prolong its useful life – potentially for years – with a more adjustable fit is to turn it into a pinafore-style apron. The basic principle is to remove the back of the dress, or a large section of it, so that the front part remains intact. Any sleeves or straps will also need to go. Use any leftover fabric to create ties that fasten the pinafore around the waist and around the neck instead. This is a trick that will also work with skirts, which can be turned into skirt-aprons in the same way.

-- Tag lines --

Whether for a golden labrador, a Persian kitten or a Bengal tiger, a good collar is the best accessory to set off one of this season's healthy, shiny coats. Make one by cutting down an old belt and lining it with a strip of felt or for a day-to-night look, try sewing a reflective strip onto a length of webbing salvaged from an old luggage strap. Another option is to refashion a lanyard name tag left over from a business conference or music festival (remove or change the name tag first). Measure the neck of the animal before cutting anything down and consider choosing a buckle that will snap open under pressure should Tibbles ever get stuck up a tree. If making a dog collar, slip on an O-ring or D-ring before fastening it, so there is something to clip the lead to when it comes to walkies.

Big is beautiful, small is beautiful. Someone should start a campaign to show that middling proportions can be beautiful too because, at the end of the day, it's all relative: when a voluminous new cashmere sweater accidentally comes out of the wash looking like it was made for a very, very tiny person then that is usually relatively bad. If there is a very, very tiny person in the household who might put that sweater to use then that is relatively better. But if the whole shrinkage operation was done on purpose in the first place – perhaps the garment wasn't really working in its original size, and maybe it even had a small snag in it or the moths had got at it or maybe a little person in the household needed an extra layer – then that is relatively brilliant for all involved.

Knowing how to shrink garments deliberately is useful and the key, very often, is heat. Depending on the material (wool and cashmere are especially susceptible to shrinkage), hot water is usually the first step. So begin by washing the garment in very hot water. If the fabric is printed it's a good idea to add baking soda to the water to preserve any writing or illustrations.

More shrinkage can then be arranged by drying the garment in a very hot dryer, leaving it to cool a little in the dryer for a few minutes before taking it out and checking the size. If it is still too big put it in the dryer again at a very hot temperature.

Another trick is to iron the garment with a hot iron as soon as it comes out of the washing machine and is still almost dripping wet. Iron towards the centre from the edges so as not to stretch the garment in the process and maintain the best shape. When it's nearly dry, put it in the dryer on a hot cycle for good measure.

Mix and match these techniques according to the fabric in question and the level of shrinkage required. For example, as silk is usually not machine washable, it is best to handwash it cool before air drying it in the sun and then putting it in the dryer just when it is still only slightly damp. Keep an eye on the dryer with all garments, checking on the size every few minutes and watch out for felting items as some materials – pure wool especially – will come out stiff.

RESOURCES

Fabric files, care and storage, further reading,
acknowledgments, picture credits and index

Silk

Handwashing is recommended for silk, using a very mild detergent (substitute any that contain bleaches or brighteners for baby shampoo) in warm water. Only soak for a few minutes at most and use a little white vinegar in the rinse water to remove any last residues of soap. Consider also using hair conditioner for an extra silky texture. After rinsing, roll the garment in a towel before hanging it to dry – wringing or twisting it will damage the weave.

Silk can be ironed, but wrinkles will also fall out of their own accord if the piece is hung up overnight, and a steamy bathroom can be a brilliantly quick fix for smoothing out crumpled garments when travelling. If you want to dry silk quickly, don't be tempted to put it in a hot dryer which will dull the fabric and risk friction damage. Instead a hairdryer on a cool setting can do the job.

Wool / Felt

Have you ever wondered how sheep keep themselves clean? As it happens, there's no need for a baaath-time rota down on the farm because wool repels dirt and water naturally. This may explain why Prince Charles' valet allegedly claims that the royal suits shouldn't need to be cleaned more than once a year, instead the clothing can simply be brushed (using a soft-bristled brush) and steamed before being put away.

Liquid spills should be wiped off immediately, while food stains can be scraped off or spot cleaned with a damp cloth or a small-pored sponge such as those used for makeup. Where wool clothes are designed for extreme outdoor use or do get visibly dirty, they should be washed cool in a mild detergent and dried on a flat surface, ideally on a mesh screen.

The downside of this wonder-fabric is its attractiveness to pests during the spring and summer months. The best way to store woollen garments to avoid their being munched on by moths is to bag them in light, cloth storage bags or keep them in cedar-wood chests or cupboards – the smell will repel the insects. A mesh bag of cedar chips or a cedar-stuffed clothes hanger used inside a closed container will also work.

Suede / Leather

As natural materials that can develop a patina and improve with age, leather and suede ought to be regularly cleaned and cared for in order to prolong their life and minimize damage. Seasonal garments ought to be cleaned both at the start and end of the wear season, otherwise once or twice a month should be enough. For light soiling and general wear, leather can be wiped down with a damp cloth and allowed to air dry. For a more thorough job, try saddle soap, before giving it a good coat of quality leather polish in order to keep the leather soft and semi-waterproof. For more serious marks and soiling, seek advice from a professional leather cleaner.

With suede, the key to a long life is prevention rather than cure when it comes to dirt and damage, but the first tool to hand when removing stains and watermarks should be a soft rubber or bristle brush, or a wire suede brush. If that doesn't work try a damp sponge or cloth, but never use chemical fluid or spot remover on suede. If you're still looking at marks after these steps, then try rubbing the area lightly with an emery board and then steam it over a boiling kettle.

For grease and fat stains, cover the mark with talcum powder and leave overnight before brushing it clean in the morning – the powder ought to absorb the grease. Makeup stains on suede can often be removed by rubbing with a piece of stale bread. When storing leather and suede, the main thing to ensure is that it will stay very dry as these materials are prone to mould.

Linen

Linen is probably the world's oldest natural fibre, pre-dating cotton and wool with records of its use going back to around 8,000 BC. Ancient Egyptians made such fine linens that modern methods are still struggling to replicate them. Dry cleaners didn't feature much in hieroglyphics, reassuringly, and linen remains universally one of the most practical fabrics when it comes to washing. The more linen is washed, the softer it becomes.

That said, it's always best to treat stains immediately where possible, and a mild detergent in cold or warm, and preferably soft, water is still to be recommended. If washing by hand, as with silk, try using a little white vinegar in the rinse water to remove soap residues.

When drying, bright sunlight will help kill bacteria and restore the fresh linen smell that's so appealing, but don't overdo it – in fact, it's advisable to bring it off the line while it is still damp as if it dries too thoroughly it can become stiff and brittle. Iron white linen hot, on both sides, but dark linen only on the wrong side.

Store linen in cloth rather than plastic bags, and avoid cardboard boxes and cedar chests as cedar contains an acid that can weaken certain cotton, linen and rayon fibres. Lavender, rosemary and rose petals are all good moth repellents.

Hemp

Hemp, like linen and leather, generally improves and gets softer with regular use and lots of laundering, so is also good to look for in second-hand and vintage shops. While not quite bulletproof, it is amazingly strong and can happily withstand extreme water temperatures and industrial cleaning processes and it dries quickly in the open air. Stretch a damp article to its natural size and shape before ironing as linen.

Naturally mothproof, hemp can be stored without risk of weevil evils, but try to avoid drying cupboards with heated pipes or cedar-lined chests as these may cause discolouration.

Synthetics

The advantages of most synthetic fabrics – including nylon, polyester, acrylics, rayon and lycra – are their strength, colour fastness and wrinkle resistance. But they do have their disadvantages as they often stain and pill easily, and lose their shape through wear and washing. Handwashing and cool ironing are usually recommended to prolong the life of synthetic garments. Always read and adhere to the instructions on the labels as blends and mixes, in particular, will come with all manner of cleaning combinations.

The first rule of resourcefulness is looking after what you already have. The useful life of garments and accessories can be much prolonged with careful care and storage.

Separate seasonal clothes and accessories and put away what's not needed for a few months safely in a cupboard to create more space and less clutter in the wardrobe.

Polishing shoes

Military technology and innovation has had much to teach the world when it comes to practicality, durability and organization, and shiny shoes are right at the top of the list. Polishing is a necessary part of properly caring for and maintaining a pair of leather shoes or boots, helping to moisturize and waterproof them, as well as adding smoothness and shine.

First use an old towel or newspaper to cover the area on which you will be working. Shoe polish is extraordinarily hard to get out of a carpet. Then begin by cleaning the dust and dirt off your boots with a damp rag. Allow them time to dry before applying a generous amount of polish using a shoe-polish brush. It will then take 15 minutes for the polish to dry before you can brush it off vigorously using a horsehair shine brush. For extra shine, spend time focusing on the toe and heel, applying another fine layer of polish with a damp cotton bud using small circular motions. Remove it again and repeat until you have a shine in which your general can see his face.

Leather boots and shoes

Leather items should only be put away after being thoroughly cleaned and polished. They will also benefit from stuffing in order to help them keep their shape and wick away any moisture. Scrunched-up newspaper, egg cartons, tubes of cardboard, rolled-up magazines and winter socks (optionally, for the very keen, these can be filled with baking soda) are all an effective alternative to shop-bought shoe and boot lasts. Once stuffed, place in a large shoebox to keep dust to a minimum and make for easy stacking.

Hats

For hats to have a long life, they need to be looked after carefully. Only clean hands should be used to handle them and the proper way to pick them up is from underneath, holding both the front and back brims. Ideally, when not in use, they should be stored in a box, on a hat stand or on a block (keep them out of direct sunlight), but at the very least they should be kept on wall hooks – hats should not be rested on flat surfaces to avoid deforming the shape of the brim. Whether vintage or contemporary, a felt hat should be brushed after every wear using a soft-bristled brush, while a damp towel is also useful for removing dust. Straw hats and panama hats that have become misshapen can often be reshaped after steaming over a boiling kettle for a few seconds.

Further Reading

Books:

Baumgartel, B.
The Complete Book of Sewing: Essential Tips and Techniques for You and Your Home
Apple Press, London
2009

Black, S.
Eco-Chic
Black Dog Publishing, London
2011

Blakeney, J., F. Blakeney, A. Livakovik and E. Schultz
99 Ways to Cut, Sew, Trim & Tie Your T-Shirt into Something Special
(see also *99 Ways to Cut, Sew & Deck Out Your Denim*)
Potter Craft, New York
2006

Blanchard, T.
Green is the New Black: How to Change the World with Style
Hodder & Stoughton, London and William Morrow/HarperCollins Publishers, New York
2008

Bolton, A. and H. Koda
Alexander McQueen: Savage Beauty
Yale University Press, New Haven and London
2011

Butterfield, C. and M.
Vintage Fashion Sourcebook
Carlton Books, London
2011

Dimant, E.
Minimalism in Fashion: Reduction in the Postmodern Era
Collins Design, New York
2010

Fletcher, K.
Sustainable Fashion and Textiles: Design Journeys
Earthscan, London and Sterling, VI
2008

Fukai, A., B. Vinken, S. Frankel, H. Kurino and R. Nii
Future Beauty: 30 Years of Japanese Fashion
Merrell, London
2011

Hollahan, L.
How to Use, Adapt and Design Sewing Patterns
A & C Black, London
2010

Knight, L.
The Dressmaker's Technique Bible: A Complete Guide to Fashion Sewing
David & Charles, Newton Abbot and Krause Publications, Iola, WI
2008

McDonald, C.
Vogue Sewing
Sixth & Spring, New York
2006

Margiela, M.
Maison Martin Margiela
Rizzoli International Publications, New York
2009

Martin, R.
The Fashion Book
Phaidon, London
2001

Nakamichi, T.
Pattern Magic
Laurence King, London
2010

Norris, L.
Recycling Indian Clothing: Global Contexts of Reuse and Value
Indiana University Press, Bloomington, IN
2010

Sanders, A. and K. Seager
Junky Styling: Wardrobe Surgery
A & C Black, London
2009

Stevenson, N. J.
The Chronology of Fashion
A & C Black, London
2011

Walker, H.
Less is More: Minimalism in Fashion
Merrell, London
2010

Wilcox, C.
Vivienne Westwood
V&A Publications, London
2005

Wolff, C., R. Fanning and R. Cooke
The Art of Manipulating Fabric
Chilton Book Co., Radnor, PA
1996

Magazines:
Amelia's Magazine
Cut Magazine (German)
Dazed & Confused
i-D
Papierdoll
SIX Magazine
Tank
Vogue

Websites:
ameliasmagazine.com
coolhunting.com
ebay.com
eco-age.com
ecouterre.com
etsy.com
instructables.com
threadbanger.com
treehugger.com

Acknowledgments

Henrietta Thompson would like to thank Sara Henrichs and Veronica Crespi for their help in making *Remake It: Clothes*, and to Neal and Emmi for being so wonderful to work with. Also a big thank you to Jubi, Alan, Olivia, Angus, Oscar and everyone else who tirelessly came up with suggestions, blindly entrusted their kit, modelled the results and generally acted enthusiastically during the making of this book.

Neal Whittington would like to thank Mum, Dad and Mark.

Picture Credits

Key:

a = above
b = below
c = centre
l = left
r = right

16–17 Dresses by Gary Harvey; photos Robert Decelis; model Tabitha @ Models 1

18–19 We are ULTRA

22 Designs by Angelene Fenuta; photos Carla Silva; hair and makeup Vanessa Jarman; styling Nadia Naeme-El Zein; models Drea Vujovic and Courtney French (NEXT)

28–31 wrk-shp, 'Building Clothes', Autumn/Winter 2011/2012; photos Jordan Duvall (jordanduvall.com)

32–33 All garments by Minna; photos François Rocquemont (francoisrocquemont.com) and Karoliina Bärlund (karoliinabarlund.com); makeup Lucy Allen

38–41 Zarth & Van der Borgh, Mirjana Rukavina and Elvira Faltermaier

42–44 Autumn/Winter 2010/2011: Christoph Musiol; Spring/Summer 2012: Jule Felice Frommelt; Autumn/Winter 2011/2012: Jule Felice Frommelt

50–51 Designs by Christopher Raeburn

52, 53, 55 Kimono Collection by Beautiful Soul www.beautiful-soul.co.uk

54 Kimono Collection by Beautiful Soul www.beautiful-soul.co.uk. Photo Christopher Dadey

58–59 Images © antiform 2011; photos Sally Cole

66–67 Rachel Freire with ECCO Leather; photos Grant Thomas

68–69 Prophetik by Jeff Garner © Christopher Dadey

75l Sinking Night, 2008; photo Jessica Cassar

75r Traces, 2011; photo Jessica Cassar

82–85 Photos Ali Kepenek; model Hanne Brüning @ Mega Model Agency

86, 87a Autumn/Winter 2011/2012; photos Jessica Bonham; styling Carley Hague; makeup Emily Wong

87b Autumn/Winter 2010/2011; photos Jessica Bonham; styling Carley Hague; makeup Emily Wong

97 Minimal Seam Construction (2010); photos Thomas McQuillan and Rob Matthews

98–99 Autumn/Winter 2010/2011: Christoph Musiol; Spring/Summer 2012: Jule Felice Frommelt; Autumn/Winter 2011/2012: Jule Felice Frommelt

101 Dr Noki

106 Endurance shirt, 2009, garment and pattern by Timo Rissanen; photos Silversalt

107 MLS Pyjamas, 2011, garments and pattern by Timo Rissanen

108–109 Habiliments (2010), Julia Lumsden. Wool, cotton, polyester, metal. Private Collection, Wellington, New Zealand

112a Autumn/Winter 2011/2012 Hooded bomber jacket

112b Autumn/Winter 2011/2012 Freestyle lapel

113al Autumn/Winter 2011/2012 Lapel hooded jacket

113ar Autumn/Winter 2011/2012 Hooded waistcoat

113bl Ladder trousers

113bc Autumn/Winter 2011/2012 Cuff edge trousers

113br Cross hood jacket suit harems

114–15 Christopher Raeburn

116 Alabama Chanin: Robert Rausch

118 Photos Christopher Dadey

126–27 A-POC Queen, 1998: animation Pascal Roulin; A-POC Cotton Baguette, 1999: animation Pascal Roulin

128 All products are the original design work of Julia Crew and handmade by Julia Crew. Photos Julia Crew and Francisco Rivotti

133 A.P.C. Butler, Worn Out Series, Jeans. Photos Olivier Placet for A.P.C.

138 Emiliana. Designed by Emiliana Design (Ana Mir + Emili Padrós)

146–49 Photos Mark Andreani and Ethan Allen Hall

169 Bernstock Speirs

170–71 All designs are original designs by Maria Papadimitriou for Plastic Seconds. All rights reserved. Images by Maria Papadimitriou

172 FENTON mixed media chain, crystal and speaker wire tassel necklace

173 Margot Bowman

176–79 Bluemâchéshoes, 2003, Greenmâchéshoes 2003, by Marloes ten Bhömer

182–83 Product photos Shannon South; model photos Evan Browning; model Johanna Bjork

190–91 sagensweden. com. Designer and owner Elin Sigrén; styling Susanna Stankierwicz; photos Werner Nystrand; model Agnes Almaqvist

192 Bethan Laura Wood

193 Henrik Vibskov

194–95 Plastic Gold (2010), Florie Salnot, Dominic Tschudin and Anne Schuhmann

198al Woman's bag (September 2010)

198ar Working laptop bag (February 2009)

198c Beauty bag (September 2011)

198bl Weekend bag (April 2010)

199 © Leigh McAlea / TRAID

204–205 Design by Joomi Lim; photos Xavier Ricolfi

206–207 Photo Guli Cohen

208 Images of recycled scarves

209al Multi Rings (2011), 209ar Rock ring (2011), 209c Stacked Bangles (2011), 209b Lace Dyed Blue Rock Bangle Close Up (2011) all by Bridget Harvey

216–17 Shoes by Hetty Rose Limited

218–19 Photos Guillermo Gómez

226 Fortune Cookie Coin Purse (2011) designed by Diana Eng (dianaeng. com); photos Douglas Eng

228–29 glovedup.com

239 Photos Minna Hepburn

240–41 Photos Alexander Malecki and Uta Neumann for Pamoyo

252–55 © Clothkits Ltd 2011, clothkits.co.uk